The Dancer's Companion

THE DANCER'S COMPANION

The
Indispensable Guide
to Getting the Most
Out of Dance Classes

BY TERI LOREN

THE DIAL PRESS / NEW YORK

Published by
The Dial Press
1 Dag Hammarskjold Plaza
New York, New York 10017

Manufactured in the United States of America

First printing

Design by Francesca Belanger

Library of Congress Cataloging in Publication Data

Loren, Teri.
The dancer's companion.

Bibliography: p.
Includes index.
1. Dancing—Study and teaching.   I. Title.
GV1753.5.L67   793.3'07   78-5624
ISBN 0-8037-1680-X
ISBN 0-8037-1681-8 pbk.

To James Waring

Haynes Owens helped create this book through his review and critique of the manuscript in draft form and by setting the inspiring example of a superb teacher.

My thanks also for support and inspiration to Arlene Rothlein, Ernestine Stodelle, Paul Sanasardo, Toby Armour, Matthew Israel, Dick and Jill Gutman, Sharon Squire, Sandra Bendayan, Andrew Goodman, and Tom, Faye, and Ben Lucatorto.

CONTENTS

FOREWORD

When I first began dancing, I spent two months in an advanced-level ballet class because I thought it was the intermediate group. There was a misprint on the school's schedule, and nobody bothered to tell me I was in the wrong class. As I hadn't been dancing very long, I didn't know the difference; I thought perhaps classes were supposed to be that hard. It wasn't until I became friendly with some of the other students that I found out I had been attempting a class in which most of the dancers were five-year veterans.

Then there was the time after I'd been dancing a while longer when I bought a pair of ballet shoes that were much too large. I tried to adjust them by tightening the strings that ran around the tops, put them on for class, and wore them for a full hour and a half. The strings were uncomfortably tight, but I didn't realize the damage I'd done until the following day, when I tried to get out of bed. The doctor diagnosed an injured Achilles' tendon, and even now I still limp through the first few steps I take each morning.

I must have danced for at least four years before I found out how to do a plié correctly. As any neophyte dancer knows, a plié is simply bending your knees, but there are so many wrong ways to do it that it isn't as easy as it sounds. I must have gone through every possible variation before the light dawned, and that happened only after I'd studied some anatomy and could visualize the joints and muscles in action during a plié. These were just a few of the hurdles I crossed en route to dancing with the companies of James Waring and Paul Sanasardo. And when I've compared notes with other dancers, I've heard similar stories and found that my experiences were not that unusual. As I think back on it, I keep reaching the same conclusion: Had I understood more about studying dance, I could have progressed more quickly than I did, I could have avoided some injuries, and I might not have had to take three years off from dancing.

Although I stayed away for a while, I came back to dancing in the end because there is simply nothing else like it. The many extraordinary teachers, choreographers, and dancers I have worked with have shown me that nothing else can so totally involve and benefit your entire mental, physical, and spiritual being. I have written this book because, as a performer, a teacher, and a student, I want to share with other dance students the ways I have learned to organize dance training better and to experience the joys of dancing more fully.

The Dancer's Companion

INTRODUCTION

Maria Montessori, the celebrated educator and creator of the Montessori method, was noted for her work with retarded children in Italy. Through a carefully designed program of self-education and sensory training, she raised the IQ's of children living in Italian slums from the retarded level to the average. How marvelous, people said, to have performed such a miracle! On the contrary, said Montessori. How unfortunate that we have so few programs for our average or our gifted students to develop *their* potential to a higher degree.

If we take an objective look at dance training as it exists today, it becomes clear that dance students, too—of all ages and all levels of ability—have very few programs available to them to ensure their development. Relatively little is done in any organized way to diagnose or foster talent, and students are left principally to their own devices to figure out what dancing is all about. Generally they have the standard equipment to cope with the world, and in an ordinary dance class can be expected to do reasonably well without much special attention. With a little luck, they come out dancing, and with a little extra talent or the good fortune of a strong and flexible body or an exceptional teacher, some come out dancing very well. For the most part, though, regardless of a student's basic capabilities, dance training is a chancy affair, and even the very talented may miss out because they never find the right route to their goals.

The Dancer's Companion answers the need of every dance student—teen-ager or adult, average or gifted, amateur or aspiring professional, beginner, intermediate, or advanced—to make dance training more organized. It is, in a way, like the Montessori method, the foundation for a special program or course that every dancer may chart for him or herself, designed to pay off in the development of each individual's dance potential. Instead of leaving students to chance devices, it gives them specific information they themselves may use to actively direct their studies. It fills in the gaps and helps students to find and put together the experiences that will make the most of their talents.

Of course, some special dance training programs do exist. In countries such as Russia, for example, there are state schools affiliated with professional companies at which dancers are rigorously prepared for a performing career from childhood. In the United States there are no such state-run schools, but we do have special summer programs and classes that are the selection and training grounds for the major performing companies.* The number of students who can be placed in these is small, unfortunately, leaving out many who might evolve into fine performers given the right conditions.

Then there's the fact that even though professional schools often conduct "open" classes (in addition to those for students being groomed for the company), they may still be geared for budding performers. You, as a student, however, may not be interested in a performing career. You may dance purely for enjoyment or to keep in shape or because you want to know more

---

* For example, there are special programs at the School of American Ballet for future members of the New York City Ballet; at the American Ballet Center for the Joffrey Ballet; at the American Ballet Theatre Company's school; at the San Francisco Ballet School; at the Alvin Ailey School; at the Martha Graham School; and so on.

about dance as an art form. It would indeed be unfortunate if you could not develop your dancing to a level that reflected your potential, regardless of whether you were striving for technical excellence, closer contact with your physical self, or simply a trimmer figure.

The Dancer's Companion is designed to help you keep sight of your own dance goals, whatever they may be, and to locate and make full use of all the resources that are at your disposal to achieve these goals. Every dance student, like every person, is unique and develops best when training fits that uniqueness as closely as possible. The Dancer's Companion enables you to identify your special aims and abilities and find the dance experiences that will match them.

Would you be just as well off if you simply concentrated on finding a good school and a good teacher, put yourself in their expert hands, and didn't spend time worrying about your uniqueness? Certainly a school and teacher are important variables in learning, and more good ones are available now that interest in dance is burgeoning. By the sheer weight of numbers, dance training is improving, and consequently you have the option among many different styles and contexts for dancing. In fact, as a student you have a better chance now than ever before of finding a ready-made environment that will come very close to suiting your needs and objectives. But even when you do locate a good school and teacher, you must still know how to make the most of them. No teacher and no school, no matter how fine, will ever live inside your body, your personality, and your learning style. If you hope to realize a return on the investments of time, money, and energy you put into dance classes, you are the one who must ultimately take charge of yourself. Even the best teacher won't enable you to realize your dance potential unless you yourself can:

● effectively evaluate a class to be sure it's suited to your interests, needs, and abilities

- attend to your own dance "housekeeping" chores, such as dress, nutrition, and rest
- work your body correctly to minimize stresses, strains, and potential injuries
- adjust to environmental conditions such as crowdedness and the size, shape, and floor of the studio, and use the barre and mirrors correctly
- participate harmoniously in class by following some standard policies and practices
- make constructive use of the teacher's corrections
- handle the psychological barriers that could stand in your way
- integrate your mind and body
- identify what you might do beyond spending time in classes to meet your dance goals

The Dancer's Companion helps you meet all these objectives. In addition, because the dance-student population has been growing dramatically each year, this book contains chapters addressed to the large number of beginning dancers and to children and adults who need special information. The enrollment of dance students in academic institutions is on the rise as well, and in recognition of this mushrooming group, *The Dancer's Companion* has a chapter on dance in colleges and universities.

In this time of assertiveness training, liberation, school-board reform, and consumer awareness, it does seem strange that dance training has remained relatively untouched. Perhaps it goes back to the historical association of dance with the ethereal ballerina—the Sleeping Beauty who waits passively for her Prince Charming. Perhaps it has something to do with attitudes that have dominated dance classes for years—attitudes that establish the teacher as the absolute authority figure in a less-than-democratic milieu. Perhaps it reflects the fact that as a dance student you *are* dependent on your teachers to a large extent— because you can't see yourself from the outside the way they can.

But it's clear that the delicate, birdlike ballerina doing all the strenuous dancing in a ballet has a very aggressive set of muscles; democracy is in; and your view of yourself is at least as important as the one your teacher has of you. As dancers and as people we are all ultimately responsible for ourselves, and there's no reason not to apply this truth to dancing. Of course, it never hurts to have a little help, and *The Dancer's Companion* is meant to provide just that: the kind of information you need to study successfully in the demanding but rewarding world of dance.

1

Choose Wisely, Choose Well: Selecting Dance Classes

When you step into a dance class, you immediately have several things in common with everyone else there. You are all about to make your hearts pump faster and increase circulation; send a better blood supply to your brains and perk up your mental processes; fill your lungs deeply with refreshing oxygen that will travel throughout your bodies; build strength, flexibility, and coordination; develop self-confidence in moving; and generally encourage the blossoming of your physical and mental well-being.

These are the basic benefits that dance classes offer any takers, and they're likely to account for many of the reasons that people love to dance. But there's more. Anyone who has a business career will tell you that a couple of dance classes a week make it easier to tackle the mental and emotional strains of work at the office. Physical-fitness experts recommend dance as an excellent all-around way to keep in shape. And the fashion industry, with a vested interest in having people look their best and take pride in their physical selves, touts the benefits of dancing, as well.

Ordinary physical exercise can do almost as much for you as dancing will, but dancing has an extra something that surpasses pure physical involvement and is fundamental to the human spirit. Through its rhythms and expressiveness, dancing can reach to the very core of your being, whether you take ballet or tap; whether it's your career or your form of recreation; or whether you've danced all your life or have just begun. Dancing can infinitely stretch your horizons of pleasure and your enjoyment of life, because it speaks to your aesthetic senses and to your spirit at the same time it addresses the physical side of your nature.

Whatever your reasons for dancing, the benefits and pleasures will always be there for you. To do you the most good, though, the classes you take must match your specific needs and goals as closely as possible. A dancer who performs (or who expects to perform) needs classes that will serve as preparation for the stage. A beginner needs classes that will lay the foundations of strength, flexibility, and coordination that dancing requires. More advanced students need classes that present the challenges that will help them continue making progress.

It would be wonderful if you could simply step into a dance studio and order up two pounds of stage presence, a yard of coordination, and four quarts of progress. Unfortunately, you can't assess your needs that way, and neither can you evaluate classes that way. Besides, taking class is an extremely personal affair. What measures up for a friend, even one who seems to have the same needs as you do, may not measure up for you.

There are many different ways to study dance, and many types of dance to choose from. There's no one "right" way to do it, only what's right for you. Here, then, are some things you need to know and think about to select the dance classes that will best suit your abilities, needs, interests, and goals.

Classes in Ballet, Modern, Jazz, and Tap

If people study dance at all, they very often choose ballet, modern, jazz, or tap. Generally speaking, there is substantial popular demand for these four types of dance classes. Possibly it's because these forms of dance have had a great deal of exposure in theaters, opera houses, movies, musical comedy, and on television.

All dancers need to take classes, whether they're beginners or professionals. Classes build and maintain the strength, flexibility, and coordination that dancing demands, and unless you take them regularly you can't expect to continue developing your dance ability. Dancers never stop taking classes, no matter how advanced or famous they become, because as soon as you stop classes, even for just a few days, your body begins to get out of shape. If you keep up classes consistently, however, you are rewarded with increasing control of your body, thereby freeing it for increasingly expressive movement.

People sometimes ask why, once you know all the dance exercises you're supposed to do, you can't simply go through them on your own and keep in shape without going to classes. The reason you can't is that you need an "outside eye"—a teacher— to keep you working correctly. You can't see yourself from the outside the way your teacher can, and without his or her help you can develop bad habits.

Classes in ballet, modern, jazz, and tap all aim to provide the outside eye, body conditioning, and other experiences you need to build the foundation for the particular type of dance you want to do. Obviously, if you're already on your way to becoming a professional ballet dancer, you've made your choice among the four types. But if you're just beginning and not exactly sure which kind of class would be best for you, or if you'd like to try something different from the classes you've been taking, the information that follows should help you choose.

BALLET CLASSES

If you opt for ballet classes, you've chosen a very exacting discipline that will make your body exceptionally strong and lithe, and that can serve as an excellent foundation for all types of body movement. You'll have to learn some new languages in ballet: the French names for positions and steps, for one; and a new movement vocabulary that might not feel immediately "natural" to your body, for another.

Ballet has a set of positions and steps that are universal; all ballet classes use them. For example, "first position," with the heels together and toes out to the side, is first position in all schools of ballet, whether in New York, Chicago, San Francisco, Moscow, or Tokyo. There are also traditionally three sections to the class: You begin with some small, localized exercises while you stand with your hand on a "barre" (a long wooden or metal handrail that runs parallel to the floor a bit above waist height); then you stand in the center of the floor for the next part of class and do bigger movements; finally you do jumps and very large steps that travel across the floor.

Although the basics are just about the same in all ballet classes, there are some variations depending on the style of ballet being taught. As you can imagine, because dance is a dynamic art, styles don't remain static. They change over the years, one style borrows from another, and some, like the American style, are mixtures of many changing ideas about dance and training.

When it comes to training, you'll find that any one style of ballet has a system of teaching that goes along with it. The system is referred to as a "technique" or a "method," so that you'll hear about classes in "Cecchetti technique," "Vaganova technique," "Bournonville method," and so on. To perform a particular style of ballet, you need technique training that corresponds to it. For example, the Kirov Ballet in Russia has a style that is quiet and restrained, brilliant but disciplined. The Bolshoi, by contrast, is flamboyant and athletic. To dance in these styles, a dancer must be trained by the right method or technique.

Aside from classes in which the technique or method is identified, you'll also hear about classes that are called simply "Ballet." These may be a mixture of styles or a particular teacher's interpretation of one, or they may be the kind of class that focuses on the basic anatomical and physical principles that support all ballet dancing in general.

For the purpose of taking classes at a beginning level, you needn't worry too much about style. Unless someone has recommended that you study one in particular, just concentrate on finding a good, straightforward class where the emphasis is on clarity, precision, and correct body mechanics. (Later in this chapter there'll be some guidelines on the things to look for.) So long as you learn these, you'll be able to adapt to any style you might later want to study. Should you decide to join a specific ballet company, you'll need classes in the style the company employs. By that time, though, you'll know more about it and will want to attend the company school, where the right style is taught anyway.

After you've reached a certain level of ability in ballet, you're likely to begin special types of class work. Three of these specialties are: pointe work—usually for women, in which you dance in pointe shoes on your toes; adagio—in which you work with a partner; and men's steps—like big jumps and turns in the air that men (and not women) normally perform on stage. Teachers sometimes give these specialties at the end of a regular class, although often a separate class is devoted to them.

The study of ballet has much to recommend it. When taught

well, it builds strength, stretch, and good body mechanics that will be useful to you in any other type of dance you may want to study. Even if you lean toward modern dance or jazz, ballet classes will help you.

MODERN DANCE CLASSES

You'll often hear people talk about modern dance in contrast to ballet. One of the reasons is that modern dance developed as a reaction against ballet. Its founders and innovators—Isadora Duncan, Loie Fuller, Mary Wigman, Hanya Holm, Ruth St. Denis, Ted Shawn, Doris Humphrey, Charles Weidman, Martha Graham—looked for new ways to dance and to break what they considered to be the artificial mold of ballet. They went back to nature and to "natural movement" and built their dancing from these roots.

The results were drastically different from ballet. And the results of one modern dance innovator were quite different from those of another. The style of dance developed by Martha Graham, for instance, looks very little like that of Isadora Duncan.

Many classes in modern dance teach the style of one of the original innovators or of a choreographer who has developed another style along the way. Some of the training that you'll find in modern dance styles are: Graham technique, Humphrey-Weidman technique, Limon technique, Hawkins technique, Horton technique, and Cunningham technique.

In the spirit of modern dance, which is to experiment with movement and not restrict it to what's been done before, new styles or variations on them spring up all the time. For instance, there are now some variations of Cunningham technique (like Viola Farber's and Gus Solomons's). And you'll recognize others who are associated with various modern dance styles or variations on them: Anna Sokolow, Ann Halprin, Paul Taylor, Daniel Nagrin, and Alwin Nikolais, to name just a few.

A choreographer or teacher may also take a little of this from one style and a little of that from another, adding his or her own ideas about movement and training to the mixture. Presto, you have yet another type of modern dance class. To make matters even more interesting, some teachers conduct classes that are a combination of ballet and modern dance, mixing types and styles to turn out a sometimes very unusual concoction.

Because the technique taught in one modern dance class can be very different from the next, you'll most likely want to look around a bit and try a few before you decide on any. You'll find the differences quite substantial. They'll determine such things as how you use parts of your body, the movements you do, and whether you spend the first, "warming-up" part of the class sitting on the floor or standing. They will also affect your whole outlook on dancing.

While you'll find modern dance classes different from each other, you'll also notice how modern dance is different from ballet. There's the way you use your back and chest, for instance. In ballet you keep your back straight and hold your chest high most of the time. In modern dance you also bend, curve, twist, and contract. Your feet are supposed to be pointed whenever they're off the floor in ballet class. In modern they're as likely to be flexed or relaxed as they are to be pointed. Then there's the way you use your leg in the hip socket; for ballet you turn it out; for modern you might turn it in or out. Of course, in ballet you usually wear shoes and in modern you usually don't. And when it comes to gravity, in ballet you want to dance as though it's not there—to soar, spin, glide, and balance in defiance of it. In modern dance class you may want to make your relationship to gravity so clear that you'll lie on the floor.

By studying modern dance, whether you're a full-time dancer or a recreational one, you'll have the opportunity to experience many, many ways to move. You won't be locked into the set vocabulary of ballet. If you're after professional dance employment, this experience can considerably improve your job prospects. Musical comedy, for example, requires that you have the facility to move in any way the choreographer wants you to. And modern dance classes can help if you aspire to a ballet company, because many ballets contain movement that is not in the traditional ballet vocabulary.

Some dancers and teachers say that you won't become strong enough or develop into any kind of really good dancer—modern or other—unless you also study ballet. Perhaps that accounts for the existence of mixed modern-ballet classes. Others, though, say that modern dance classes without ballet can give you all the strength and skill you need, and that ballet can rob you of some of the relationship to gravity that's essential if you want to do modern dance really well. Most modern dancers I know do also take ballet class, and I've heard of many modern choreographers who insist that their dancers go to ballet as well as modern classes. You'll definitely want to think about it and find out what works best for you.

JAZZ CLASSES

You can enjoy yourself in almost any dance class, provided the conditions are right. But jazz classes give you such great latitude to express your own personal style that you may find you take more pleasure in them than in any other kinds of classes.

There is a vocabulary of "steps" in jazz and a traditional sequence from warm-up exercises through to big, dancy combinations of movement. There are also what you might consider to be jazz styles and systems of training (Jack Cole, Matt Mattox, Katherine Dunham, and Luigi are names you'll hear associated with them) that determine what steps you do, how you do them, and the sequence you follow in class.

Jazz dance uses many of the same kinds of strength and stretch that ballet does, and is like modern, too, in that you move your body in many nontraditional ways. Overall, jazz is a big, bold way to move that can make you feel particularly expansive and expressive.

Many people like jazz dance because it uses popular music with a good, strong beat as well as the intricate, syncopated rhythms of jazz music. Jazz looks and feels familiar, too, because people frequently see it performed on television and in musical comedy.

While jazz dance allows a lot of room for letting you express what's inside, you must build quite a bit of strength and skill before you can fully use that freedom. That's why you'll spend a good part of class on exercises to develop your muscles, flexibility, and coordination.

If you're thinking about any type of performing career, but especially musical comedy, you'll definitely want to take jazz classes. Adults who are just beginning to study will also find jazz dance especially good. You won't necessarily care about the different styles of jazz, so long as classes generally come up to your standards. (More about evaluating classes later.)

TAP CLASSES

Tap dancing is vibrant, joyful, and fun to do. Many students say it lets you forget all your troubles. Jerry Ames, who runs a tap dance studio in New York City, makes a good point by asking, "Have you ever seen a sad tap dancer?" [1]

Just about anyone can learn to tap dance, though some of the more intricate steps require concentrated practice. In fact, part of the reason that tapping takes your mind off your worries is that all your mental powers are consumed in making your feet produce the right sounds on the right beats.

A tap dance studio may at first glance seem to be much less formal than a ballet or modern dance studio. Once class starts, though, you'll find yourself paying close attention and doing some serious, hard work. But that doesn't detract from the fun you'll have in class; it just makes it that much more possible to enjoy your accomplishments.

Most of the work in tap appears to be done by your feet. That's deceiving. You have to learn a lot about relaxing your whole body and giving in to its weight to cause the tap sounds to come out correctly at the ends of your feet. Tap makes you aware of the tension factor throughout your body—when to hold and when to relax—and by doing so can help you in the other kinds of dancing you may undertake, ballet included.

You can develop strong legs and feet and a firm back and stomach by taking tap classes. You might not build as much stretch and flexibility as you'd like, however, and you may therefore want to supplement your tap classes with ballet, modern, or jazz.

Tap has been experiencing a revival lately, and is being used more and more in shows and on television. If you intend to head toward performing in these media, be sure you put a good portion of tap training under your belt. For anyone else tap may not be a necessity, but it is one fine way to get into shape and have a great time.

If you need more information before deciding whether you want to take ballet, modern, jazz, or tap classes, you should follow some of the reading and research suggestions in Chapter 13, "Beyond the Physical." You can also sample classes in a number of types, or at least the two or three you think you're most attracted to. You might even simultaneously dip into more than one class, trying modern on Tuesdays, say, and jazz on Fridays. There's no need to tie yourself up in one type of dance exclusively, not even when you're a professional. You might have one that's your main interest, but it's not a bad idea to diversify and develop a feeling for other types and styles.

Technique Levels in Dance Classes

One of the meanings for the word "technique" in dance is the amount of basic dance skill you've developed. A dancer with a "good technique" is able to execute steps well and is generally adept at moving. As a beginner, of course, your technique won't be as developed as it will be after you've had some practice. Until you've taken classes for a while, in fact, you may not have much to depend on in the way of strength, flexibility, and coordination.

To take account of students' varying needs in evolving their technique, dance classes are usually divided into levels: Beginning, intermediate, and advanced are the three main levels. Thus, you'll find classes called "Beginning Ballet," "Beginning Modern Dance," "Intermediate Tap," "Advanced Jazz," and so on.

If it seems warranted, classes are also further divided into levels and labeled with such names as: basic, fundamental, advanced beginners (usually for students who have had six months to a year of training), advanced intermediate (sometimes called "fast" intermediate, which means the class is geared to students who are more proficient than the average intermediate dancer), intermediate advanced (which would be a little "slower" than the advanced class), and professional. All these divisions and subdivisions can get pretty confusing. What's worse, an "advanced beginners" or "intermediate advanced" class as taught by one teacher may be at a very different technical level from one called by the same name but taught by another teacher. Sometimes the determining factor in the level of a class is which students show up for it that day. A good teacher always adjusts the teaching to suit the students, regardless of what's printed on the schedule.

If you've never danced before or have never taken a class in a particular type of dance, you'll know that you'll probably want to start out somewhere around the basic, fundamental, or beginner level. But your choice of a beginning-level class may also have something to do with your general physical condition. For instance, if you've danced at some time in your life but have since lapsed into being seriously out of shape, you may want to take a beginning-level class even though you once worked your way up to intermediate. On the other hand, if you've studied some modern dance and are about to start a new modern class, you may not be sure whether the beginning level is right for you. The previous modern dance style you studied may be enough like the one you're about to try to put you into the intermediate group right away.

Your best bet in deciding on a class level is to talk to the teacher or school. In many cases they'll have you take a trial class and place you in a level accordingly. You also have to judge for yourself, though. If you're taking a class and it feels "too fast" or "too slow" for you—that is, you either can't do anything very well or everything seems too easy—you should talk to the teacher. You'll also probably want to move up to the next level of class as your technique develops. If you feel you're ready for it, again, speak to your teacher.

It's very important to choose the right technical level for yourself. A class that's too advanced for you won't give you the time or opportunity to work on the basics that you need. A class that's not advanced enough won't challenge you, interest you, or spur you on to new achievements.

Classes for Adults and Children

Besides breaking groups of students down according to technical level, it's also useful to divide them on the basis of other needs. Two groups that are special in this respect are adults and children.

Adult classes are usually for people who start dancing for the first time at around the ages of eighteen to twenty-five or older, and who don't intend to have a performing career. Adult classes are for adult minds and adult bodies, even though they may be offered at the beginning, basic, or fundamental level of technique. Often adult classes are further divided into intermediate and advanced levels.

Children are grouped and taught in a way that takes their less mature minds and physiques into account, as well as their special developmental needs. Here again you will find beginning, intermediate, and advanced classes.

Since children and beginning adults are such special groups, I've devoted the next chapter to them. If you know a child who wants to take dance classes, or if you're a beginning adult, you'll find particular suggestions there.

Other Types of Classes

Many dance students have special problems with, or are particularly interested in, working on their flexibility or their body alignment. To meet their needs, teachers may set up special classes—called "Stretch Class," for instance, or "Placement Class." (Alignment is part of placement; more about this in Chapters 3, 6, and 7.)

You may also notice that there are therapeutic classes for dancers who are recovering from an injury and who need to work especially carefully.

Special classes like these are not normally offered in the ordinary school curriculum or by most independent teachers. You have to go a bit out of your way to find them when the need arises. Some of the suggestions in the next section should help you.

To give students a concentrated experience in a particular type or style of dance, a system of training, or a choreographer's special approach, you'll often find "intensive courses" offered. These are normally given during the summer or school holidays, when more students can take advantage of them. If you want a sampling of dance that you can't get anywhere else, and you have a limited time to do it in, an intensive course may be just what you're looking for. The next section will help you find these, too.

Finding Classes

Dance classes are offered under a number of arrangements. One is a "school" situation in which there'll be quite a few different classes and anywhere from one or two teachers on up. A school may give classes in just one type of dance—a "ballet school," for example—but more often the other types can also be found under the same roof.

Another situation is the one in which an independent teacher sets up shop by him or herself, not calling the base of operations a school because it's a little less formal. There are many teachers who work on their own in this way, and among them are some of the finest around. Occasionally, an independent teacher will team up with one or two other independents and they'll rent studio space together and possibly share some of the teaching load. Sometimes this kind of partnership slips into becoming a school.

A "company school" is yet another type of arrangement. Here many of the classes are given for company members or to prepare young hopefuls to join the company. Often a company school also gives classes for other types of students (children, adults, and other nonprofessionals, for instance) and offers types of dance besides the one the company performs. A ballet-company school, for example, may also offer classes in modern and jazz dance.

Although they don't operate what are officially called "company schools," many choreographers with companies of their own also teach classes. You don't have to be in the company to take classes, but if you want to perform, being in class will help you get exposure to the choreographer and may eventually lead to your dancing with the company.

How do you go about finding out where these various arrangements exist? Here are a few suggestions:

- *Word-of-mouth:* Asking other people for recommendations is an excellent way of finding out about schools and teachers. Ask among any dance students you know, your friends, and acquaintances for places they've tried and liked and that they think might be right for you. Have them describe the classes and the teachers and tell you as much as they can about them. (Incidentally, it's interesting that many teachers prefer word-of-mouth advertising to any other kind. They may not even bother with a telephone listing.)

- *Dance Magazine:* A school-and-teacher directory appears at the back of each issue of *Dance Magazine.* In addition, the publication issues a "Dance Education Directory" in their *Annual* that lists schools, teachers, colleges, and summer and intensive programs. Ads from dance schools and teachers all over the country can also be found throughout every issue of the magazine. Look for a copy at your newsstand or in your library, or write *Dance Magazine,* 10 Columbus Circle, New York, N.Y. 10019. Browse through it and note all the places that sound as though they offer the classes you're after.

- *Yellow Pages telephone directory:* The Yellow Pages for your city lists and publishes ads from dance schools and teachers. In most cities the heading to look under is "Dancing Instruction."

- *Newspaper ads:* Newspapers that have a dance page or that cover dance events may also publish ads from schools and teachers, either on the dance page itself or somewhere nearby.

- *City Guides:* Paperback directories to major cities may contain a section on "the arts." For example, a book entitled *The Creative New Yorker* by Barry Tarshis[2] contains information on dance schools in New York City. If you live in a major city, keep your eyes open for such a guide.

- *Dancers you've seen and liked:* If you particularly like a dancer you've seen perform and feel you might want to follow the same route, you can find out where he or she has studied. Look in a dance encyclopedia if the dancer is a well-known performer, or write directly to the dancer in care of the theater or the company in which he or she works. Try to find out not only where the dancer has trained but also the types or styles of dance involved. Then, if it turns out that you don't live near enough to the dancer's school or teacher, you can at least look for training in the same kinds of dance.*

In your search through directories and advertisements, you'll find that a one-line or otherwise very brief listing of a school or teacher may not tell you very much. In some cases, though, that's all that's needed. For instance, in the New York City Yellow Pages, there's an entry that reads simply "Martha Graham School of Contemporary Dance." A famous name like that is enough to give you some idea of whether you'll want to find out any more about classes.

Ads and listings that give greater detail about classes will be more useful. They often tell you the type of dance that's taught or other features of a school's offerings. Here are some examples:

Classical Ballet—Modern—Jazz—Tap—Drama; Morning —Afternoon—Evening Classes; Adults—Children—Teens —Tots; Career Women—Businessmen—College People—Teachers; Beginners—Professionals
  —*from an ad placed by the New School of Dance in the New York City Yellow Pages (1977–78 edition)*

* This is George Balanchine's idea.

The official school of DANCERS, the contemporary ballet company under the direction of Dennis Wayne. A limited number of scholarships are available.
—*from an ad for Dancer School, New York City, in* Dance Magazine *(September 1977), p. 17*

Ballet, Modern, Flamenco, Yoga, Improv, Javanese Dance, Character, Tap—taught by Professional Dancers at reasonable rates
—*from a listing for Dance Spectrum Center & Company, San Francisco, in* Dance Magazine *(September 1977), p. 108*

Of course, the more a description sounds like you, your needs, or your interests, the more likely it is that classes will fit you.

Once you've identified some schools or teachers that look like possibilities, the first thing you might want to check on is their location. If they're too far from your home, this may eliminate them entirely.

Next you should call the school or teacher and ask any of the following questions that apply to your needs:

- *What types of dance are taught? Ballet? Modern? Jazz? Tap?* This is a cross-check on the original recommendation, ad, or listing. Some places named "Ballet School" also give other classes. You may be able to take more than one type of class at the same place, if that's of interest to you.
- *Do they specialize in any styles or techniques?* You'll ask this question only if you know you especially want one in particular—for example, Cecchetti technique in ballet, Graham technique in modern, Mattox technique in jazz—or if you've already tried one technique and now want to try something different.
- *Do they offer special classes for adults? children? profes-*

sionals? Or whatever special group you belong to or are interested in. *Any intensive courses?*

- *What levels of technique are classes in?* If you don't know what level you'll want to take classes at, ask if they'll place you in a class at the right level or if you must decide for yourself.

- *Are you required to take a certain number of classes per week or to sign up for a "course of study"?* A number of schools require that you take two classes every week; in some cases you must show up for class at the same time and on the same days each week. Most independent teachers operate on a much less formal basis, letting you take the classes that fit your schedule best. It may be better for you personally to sign up for a course of study or the same classes every week, however, just because it imposes a discipline that you may not want to handle on your own. Decide for yourself whether you need the discipline or the flexibility.

- *How much are classes?* Most classes range from $3 to $5 each, with discounts depending on how many you take per week or pay for in advance. Professional discounts are offered by many schools and teachers. Find out if you have to pay for any "courses of study" in advance. See if the rates and payment schedule fit your budget.

- *Are there any other fees?* Some schools have a one-time registration fee. It may be worth it if you're convinced it's the place you want to study. If another place sounds just as good and doesn't charge a registration fee, you may want to save yourself a few dollars.

- *Are there any scholarships?* If so, how do you qualify? Many scholarships are for budding performers, though some places exchange free classes for help in running the studio (at the desk or in cleaning up, for instance).

- *Is there a performing company affiliated with the school or teacher?* If performing is your bag, also find out whether students are often taken into the company on the basis of their work in class, or if you have to audition as well.
- *How long has the school or teacher been in operation?* If you know nothing else about a place, the fact that it's been in business for any length of time is a good sign that something's being done right. Of course, a place that's new can also be good, so you won't want to eliminate it just because it hasn't been around very long.
- *Can they give you a schedule of classes?* Get a printed one if it's available; otherwise take your own notes. Be sure to check the class schedule against your own time constraints. Eliminate any classes that don't really fit in comfortably. Sometimes a schedule will also contain the "rules and regulations" of the school or describe its purposes or ideas about dance. Read it carefully to get a feeling for the tone of the place.
- *May you observe a class before taking it?* Describe your previous experience and interests and ask which one they recommend that you watch and consider taking. If they won't let you observe, ask which one you should try.

After you've done your initial research, your next step will be to evaluate the class or classes you think sound the best for you. Anyone can open a dance school in the United States. There just aren't any set rules for who is qualified. It'll be up to you to determine whether the classes are good, and you can do this by watching or taking classes.

Some schools will let you watch their classes, but many won't because they feel it creates confusion and is distracting to the students and the teacher. If you can't observe before taking a class, you may want to visit the place to get a feeling for it. You can do this under the guise of picking up a schedule or asking questions face-to-face instead of over the phone. You can often tell a lot by chatting in person with the teacher or whoever is at the reception desk. You can also glimpse the students who are around the school and decide if they are enough like you to make you feel comfortable in classes. You can look over the facilities and see if they're to your taste. A word of advice, however: Never be put off by the appearance of a dance studio. Very good classes are often conducted in very crummy-looking places. If you're the kind of student who likes to store clothes properly in a locker or to take a shower after class, you'll definitely want to check out all the facilities. But, in general, don't expect much. Accommodations in dance studios tend to be on the lean side.

If you have the chance while you're visiting, you should talk to other students and listen to what they have to say about classes.

Evaluating Classes You Observe

Provided the teacher or school gives you permission to watch, and you have the time to do it, you can evaluate the class you think you'll be taking by using the questions I've listed below. Many factors will go into making a class a good one for you, and these questions will identify a number of them. There are some elements that I feel are absolute musts, though—that reveal immediately whether the instruction in a class is going to teach anybody anything. In the list you'll see a star (☆) beside each of these essentials, and I would say that you probably shouldn't bother with a class where more than one or two don't come up to standard. Other factors, while important, won't make or break the quality of a class. If they're present, things will be that much better; if not, there may be other compensating ingredients. You can rate these elements for yourself to decide how important they are to you. To give you an example, the fact that the music sounds poor because the piano is out of tune may rank far down on your list of priorities compared with the fact that you feel you have a lot in common with the other students in the class.

It may turn out that, for your needs, the answer to just one of the questions will make up your mind. Whether your decision is based on one factor or ten, in every case you should try to put your finger on the reasons, because that's how you'll begin to learn what makes a good class for you.

Incidentally, don't worry if you think you don't know anything about dancing. You don't have to. Just watch carefully with the questions in mind.

Does the teacher

☆ *make constructive corrections?* That is, does he or she tell students what *to do* as well as what *not* to do?

☆ *sound encouraging or at least neutral whether making corrections or general remarks?* This is as opposed to sounding discouraging, negative, or unfriendly.

☆ *seem to like teaching and to be involved with and interested in teaching the students?*

☆ *keep the class moving, alive, and well paced?* Or does it seem to go in fits and starts, with long, dull periods in between bursts of activity? Sometimes this tells you whether the teacher has planned what's to come next, so that it's not necessary to stop at length and figure it out while class is in progress. Sometimes it means that the teacher is talking too much while the students have to stand still and listen.

☆ *give attention and make corrections to almost every student individually and/or to the class as a whole?* The important thing here is to notice whether everyone seems to get attention, either personalized or at least generalized, and that the teacher doesn't seem to be giving the class for only one or two students.

☆ *explain and demonstrate carefully and clearly?* This is not so important for advanced-level dancers, but is absolutely essential for beginners. If the teacher doesn't demonstrate personally in a beginners' class, there should be a more advanced student who does.

☆ *seem to have a good technique or look good when demonstrating?* Again, this is essential for beginning-level classes, though not for advanced. Whoever demonstrates should look as if he or she knows what's going on.

☆ *make clear the relationship of the music to the dancing?* When you watch a modern dance performance, the music sometimes seems to have nothing to do with the dancing. For classes, however, the connection must be obvious. The teacher should set the exercise or dance steps clearly on specific counts of the musical accompaniment. If this has been done well, you should see the students all move on the same beats, with only minor variations. Note also whether the teacher makes a point of the link between the dancing and the "spirit" or "flavor" of the music, as well as the tie to counts, measures, and phrases.

— *use his or her voice well?* When the teacher's voice is used well in class, it becomes as important as the music in making you want to dance. It doesn't matter whether the teacher's voice is deep or high, smooth or raspy; so long as it's used well, it can inspire and excite you, and teach you an enormous amount about the energy and dynamics of dancing.

— *have a personality you like or that seems to work well in the class?* Some teachers may seem too bossy to you;

others may seem too quiet or gentle. Although you may have your own personal preference, you should also notice whether you think the teacher's personality is effective in the class.

Do the students
☆ *look distorted, misaligned, or twisted to you?* This may reflect the students' basic abilities, but it also can tell you a lot about the teacher. While there are some unusual positions you may assume while dancing, none of them should violate good body mechanics. Watch the students for a clear body line that is not collapsed on one side or the other, that looks "balanced." See if their knees are straight when they're supposed to be and well bent when required. Look for a good lineup of the body on top of the legs; when the students stand in profile, see if their upper body looks as if it's leaning forward or backward off the legs most of the time. Ideally, it should look as if each part of the body is resting comfortably on top of the one below (head over the spine, shoulders over the rib cage, rib cage over the hips, hips over the legs). Note whether the teacher makes corrections to the students about these kinds of things.
☆ *look more intent than tense?* Even though they may be working hard, students shouldn't seem overwrought.
☆ *look as if they are forcing or straining a lot?* If there are many furrowed brows and clenched teeth during class, the teacher may be pushing too hard or not warming the class up well enough.
☆ *perform the movements and steps with clarity?* Or do they look "muddy"? This may be a sign of whether the teacher demonstrates clearly or explains carefully enough or is gearing the class at the right level.
— *seem to improve after the teacher makes a correction?* If so,

the teacher has obviously done a good job of noticing what's wrong and communicating how to fix it. If not, though, it doesn't always mean the opposite. Often it takes awhile for a correction to sink in.

— *run into each other a lot?* This can mean the teacher hasn't spaced students properly, isn't directing the class well, or has accepted too many students for the available space. It can be dangerous.

— *look responsive and appear to be motivated?* This may tell you whether the teacher is making the class challenging enough for the students.

— *look as if they're enjoying themselves from time to time, or at least not being continually frustrated or made unhappy?*

— *seem to be people you'd like being in class with?*

— *seem to be people whose needs or interests might be similar to yours?* If your goal is to perform, are there students who look like prospective performers? If you're in the business world, are there others who look as if they might be, too? If you're male, are there a couple of other men in the class? Having people like you in class will make you feel more comfortable and means that the class will be geared more toward your needs.

— *appear for the most part to be on approximately the same technical level?* It's good to have an advanced student or two in a beginning or intermediate class to serve as examples for other students to follow. With too many diverse levels, though, the teacher may have a rough time making exercises neither too hard nor too easy for everyone.

Does the musical accompaniment

☆ *seem right for the kind of dancing being done?* The wrong music or music that's played poorly can kill any dancing.

— *sound enjoyable to your ears?*

— *get played right away (most of the time) when the teacher asks for it?* Nothing can make a class drag more than a musician who consistently takes a long while to find the right piece of sheet music.

Does the type of movement or dancing
☆ *evoke a positive response in you?* Does it look like something you'd enjoy doing?
— *fit the expectations you had?* For instance, you might have selected a ballet class because you'd been to the ballet and felt you'd like doing it. But when you observe the beginning ballet class, you may find that the exercises don't look that appetizing. Of course, you need to do the exercises to eventually be able to execute the more exciting steps. Your expectation might have been that you'd do a lot more "dancing," though, in which case you might want to reconsider and try something else.
— *make sense to you?* That is, does there seem to be a logical progression from one thing to the next in class?

In general
— *Is the atmosphere in the class or around the school inviting?*
— *Is the place too crowded?*
— *Do the changing, bathroom, and shower facilities meet your needs?*
— *What do the students say about the class or school?*

Finally, before you leave you should find out
☆ *What is the teacher's background?* Impressive performing experience doesn't always make a good teacher; neither do academic credentials. But, generally speaking, the more dance exposure and experience a teacher has, whether it be in teaching, performing, or study, the more of an investment and interest

he or she is likely to have. This doesn't automatically make a good teacher. It does usually tip the scales a bit favorably, though.

Evaluating Classes You Take

When you can't observe a class to evaluate it, or if you're the kind of person who prefers to dive right in rather than to watch, you'll have to use a slightly different approach to making your judgments. Obviously, when you participate in class you'll experience it by doing the dancing as well as by noticing what's going on around you. By the same token, you won't be able to notice the other students and the surroundings as much because you'll be concentrating on your own dancing.

Another thing to keep in mind is that you can't always judge a class properly until you've taken it a few times. The first time you go to a new class, you may be a little nervous. You won't be sure what the teacher is going to expect, and you may wonder if you're going to do well. It can take a little time to get used to the size and shape of the studio or mirrors and windows in unfamiliar places. Then, too, in some classes all the other students may already know the standard warm-up the teacher gives, and new students will be expected to pick it up as they go along. It'll take a few classes to catch on, and it won't be fair to assess the class until you do.

You're best off evaluating a class after you've been going to it awhile. Under normal circumstances eight to ten classes with the same teacher taken on a regular basis (minimally once a week) is a good trial run. That is, unless you sense there's something wrong immediately. It may be a matter of instant chemistry between you and the teacher, or your intuition that you shouldn't have the kind of uncomfortable sensation you're experiencing in your lower back. If you decide against continuing with a class, you should try to pinpoint the exact reason why.

Understanding what makes a class wrong for you will help you find one that's right.

Sometimes you won't have the luxury of taking several classes before you commit yourself to a course of study. For instance, a number of schools may want you to make a decision about signing up for a series of ten on the basis of one trial class. While it's hard to reach an informed conclusion after just one class (unless you have that immediate feeling that it's wrong for you), your job may be easier if you keep in mind the questions I've already listed and also apply the ones that follow. You can use the questions after you've taken one class, ten classes, or at any time you think an evaluation is in order. Again, you'll see a star beside the items I think are essentials.

Did you

☆ *feel your body was distorted, misaligned, twisted, or seriously uncomfortable?* Or feel any pain in your ankles, knees, or lower back? You should be receiving instruction in the kind of good body mechanics that will enable you to work correctly, without harming your body. You should never continue to do anything that causes any kind of pain in your ankles, knees, or lower back. If the class is right for you in other ways, you should ask the teacher to work individually with you to eliminate the pain. If you can't, the type of dance or the class may be the wrong one for you.

☆ *feel you had to force yourself or your muscles to do many of the exercises or steps?* You should expect to work in class, but you shouldn't feel you have to strain excessively. If you do, the type of dancing may be wrong, or the level of the class, or it may be the method the teacher uses.

☆ *like the way the movement felt to your body? to your personality?* Dance movement that fits your body seems to flow through it. Although it might take you some time to feel it in ballet and tap classes, after you've worked at it awhile flow usually comes. Jazz and modern dance seem to fit more naturally on many bodies and personalities; they seem to be more "organic." Movement that's organic feels as though it's part of you. Some types of movement just naturally come closer to your physical and emotional self and will therefore feel more organic to you.

☆ *feel exhilarated after class rather than exhausted and down?*

☆ *follow the class reasonably well?* Were you able to do most of the exercises or steps in the right sequence most of the time? Or did you feel thoroughly like a fish out of water? Think about whether the class is at the right level for you as well as whether the type of dance is to your taste.

☆ *feel you repeated the exercises enough?* Repetition is extremely important in learning to dance. Your muscles must do the same exercises over and over again to be able ultimately to work correctly. Of course, you won't want to repeat things to the point where it becomes distasteful. You should be left with a little edge of appetite. However, you shouldn't feel you didn't get a chance to even come close to some kind of understanding.

— *feel you moved enough or had a good workout?* Don't settle for simulated dancing, where you just "float" around and go through a pale imitation of using your body.

— *find it easy to pay attention and become involved?* Generally, a class that's right for you won't bore you. Keep in mind, though, that an attention problem doesn't always lie with the class or the teacher. On some days you might just not be with it. Judge accordingly.

— *enjoy the class and get a sense of accomplishment?*
— *find yourself motivated to do the dancing?*
— *understand most of the things the teacher said?*
— *feel comfortable with the other students?* Were there enough people around your age? your level of technique? Having some people who are better than you are in class gives you a model to follow and a goal to shoot toward. But if most of the students are technically much better than you are, the class will be paced for them more than it is for you, and you're likely to miss out on the basics you need. On the other hand, if you're better than everyone else, you may not find the kind of challenges you need to make further progress.
— *find the "vibrations" right?* Was there too much tension in the atmosphere? too much competition? not enough excitement and energy?

After you've taken class for several months on a regular basis, you may also want to begin thinking about these questions:
☆ *Are you starting to derive what you want from classes?* If you're in it for body conditioning, are your muscles firming up? Is your stamina improving? Are you becoming more flexible? If you're in a class to learn more about performing, is the teacher helping you to project, to dance with assurance, and to raise your confidence level?
— *Do you find yourself generally looking forward to classes?*

It's likely that as you grow more experienced with classes, you'll develop other questions to assess factors that you think are important or that make up the essentials for you. The more precise you can be about your needs, the better the results of your classes will be.

Some Concluding Notes on Finding Good Classes for Yourself

It's said that behind every great performer there's a great teacher (and in many cases there are several). Your teacher is, in fact, a very powerful determining factor in your dance experience, whether you're a performer or not. Your teacher shapes and structures the dancing that you do and can help you immeasurably in achieving any goals you may set for yourself.

Just what makes a great teacher is not easy to define. And just who will be the right one for you personally is yet another matter. You can't take any one facet of a teacher—the ability to make excellent corrections, an encouraging approach, the ability to inspire, a keen aesthetic sense, good pacing of the class—and say that's it. A good teacher is a combination of many abilities and personal characteristics, and not all good teachers have the same ones in the same amounts. Most important, though, a teacher's abilities and characteristics must mix well with your own, and in turn with general class conditions. For example, even a very fine teacher conducting a class at your level and in the kind of dance you're crazy about won't necessarily be the right one for you if the class atmosphere is so competitive that it drives you to distraction.

Choosing the right class is further tied to your phase of development and your changing goals. You may need to switch teachers and classes as you progress or as you have new ideas about the outcome of your dance studies. If you intend to perform, you may even need to change cities to find the right teacher. (Many dancers move to New York City both for the performing opportunities and for the chance to study with some very good teachers.) Beyond that, you may want to try studying with more than one teacher at the same time to get exposure to different styles or systems of training.

Experimenting with classes doesn't mean jumping around

from one school or teacher to the next. It means testing various alternatives in an organized way, giving each one a fair trial, and knowing why you've decided it's right or wrong for you. It means being able to name specific features that account for your opinion or decision.

There is one other critical element in this whole business of choosing a class, and that is your knowing how to take class productively. The most careful and organized system of choosing isn't complete unless you also organize your approach to class. The rest of this book is devoted to helping you do just that.

2

The Questions of Age:
Children, Adults,
and Age Anxiety

. . . every human being is born to dance. It is our heritage.

—Evelyn de La Tour [3]

There's nothing wrong with dancing just for the sake of dancing, without a performing career in mind. Modern, ballet, jazz, and tap may all be seen as activities in and for themselves. There's also nothing wrong with dancing if you don't have the "perfect" dancer's body. Take a sampling of professional dancers and you'll see an enormous variety of physiques and sizes. There is no reason why anyone who wants to shouldn't dance. As I see it, it's one of your basic human rights.

As one of your rights, dancing belongs to you throughout your entire life, from the minute you're born. You can start dancing at any age, and you really don't ever have to stop. The only thing that you'll want to vary is the kind of dancing you undertake, because at different stages of your development different ways to study or do dancing will come closer to your physical, mental, and emotional needs.

Children

Although this book isn't intended for children, once you become a dance student, parents inevitably start asking you about classes for their offspring. Or you may be a parent yourself who's interested in learning the facts about dance for your child. The information that follows is meant to give you an understanding that I hope will get some of the kids you know headed in the right direction.

BEFORE CHILDREN REACH EIGHT OR TEN

Frequently when parents think of dance for their children they think of ballet. Until the age of eight, though, a child is not equipped to handle the physical and mental discipline of a true ballet class. Bones are too soft to take on the rigors of ballet, and you can seriously harm mental and emotional growth by trying to force a child under eight to concentrate with the intensity that ballet requires. Keep in mind also that eight isn't the magic age for every child; some might not be ready for ballet until they're ten, eleven, or even older.

Yes, it's true there are exceptions: "baby ballerinas" and very young kids who can do adult tricks such as spinning on their toes. Every parent likes to believe his or her child is exceptional. But there is far more danger in trying to fit a child into the ballet mold at too early an age than there is advantage to his* or her development as a dancer. Starting ballet studies too early can actually destroy any potential a child might have.

Children, especially under the age of five, don't naturally separate their physical selves from their intellectual and emotional selves. You see it when they're happy, as they jump up and down; when they're angry, as their arms and legs flail. You can see the intellect blended with the physical in the bright, shining eyes and open mouth that might express wonder at a new discovery, or the fidgeting that indicates attention has run out. Children can start taking a dance class as young as three, but under the age of eight or ten they need a form of dance study that doesn't ask them to fragment the whole that they are. They need an experience that treats the physical as an expression of their physical, mental, and emotional unity.

For children under the age of eight or ten, dancing should be something other than a traditional ballet class. It should be an activity that takes into account not only their less-mature physical, mental, and emotional characteristics, but also their special developmental needs.

Play and accomplishment. Play is critical in the development of a child. It fulfills a function that psychologists say is fundamental to the building of personality and for which there is no substitute. Thus, a child needs a dance environment that allows for play. At the same time children have a tremendous need to sense growth, to feel an ever-increasing ability to control what happens around and to them, and in particular to control their bodies. A dance experience can't be so constricting that the sense of play is lost, nor should it be so free and unstructured that there are no results the child might point to and say, I can do something with my body now that I couldn't do when I was younger.

Attention and discipline. Kids need to fool around at times; it's

* The use of the masculine pronoun isn't all wishful thinking; young boys are going to dance classes in increasing numbers.

part of their need to play and to test out the limits adults set for them. To learn, though, they need to pay a certain amount of attention. The important thing is that a child's attention be held not so much by directive but rather through the inherently involving nature of the lesson content. The environment has to be such that the child knows a certain amount of flexibility exists for his or her limited attention span; at the same time he or she must want to pay attention and follow the class routine because it is interesting.

Threats and reprimands generally don't produce good dancing for children. Imaginative devices are much more effective in encouraging them to explore movement or perform exercises.

Kids need a teacher who has a playful outlook and who will help them to be attentive and disciplined without being overbearing. There has to be a give-and-take about the determination of events in the class, and, in general, the child needs guidance rather than domination.

Energy and motion. Children have very high energy levels and they need to move. It's just not a good idea to get them stuck in positions or ask them to sit still and listen a lot. Dance class must be a place where they can get into action. Attention and discipline problems are minimized when there's enough structured physical activity.

Coordination and strength. Coordination and overall strength are different for children at various ages. Usually they can skip on one foot by the time they're three, but alternate skipping on two feet might not happen until later. To ask them to perform physical feats that are beyond their basic abilities of strength and coordination is unfair and accomplishes little except to cause frustration. But while a dance class shouldn't be far beyond a child's basic abilities, it also has to be challenging enough to keep him or her interested.

Rhythm. Rhythmic sense also needs time to evolve. A child of three usually can't clap or step in perfect time to music; an older child can. Because rhythm is so fundamental to dancing, it must be part of a dance lesson. However, the teacher's emphasis has to allow for the child's ability to cope with it.

Creativity. The dance experience for a child under ten shouldn't be aimed exclusively toward coordination, strength, and rhythm. There is a fertile field of development possible through use of the child's natural inclination to express himself or herself physically. In fact, many teachers feel that children have a basic need to make up their own dances—to bring to the outside what they experience on the inside. Whether children use technical dance skill or rhythm while creating isn't critical, but some part of the dance activity should encompass opportunities for them to make up their own unique dances.

Sociability. At three the child is ready to begin branching out of the "me" phase and into the new terrain of social interaction. Dance in pairs and in groups can take advantage of this readiness and also significantly cultivate its growth.

Adult values and tricks. A child needs to dance through his or her own body; this is of primary importance for building the physical confidence and control each child needs for dancing. Rigid standards of technique, such as those applied to performing professionals, can't be applied to a child. Children must be allowed to move in ways that are expressive for their own bodies, even though they may not precisely conform to the "ideal."

Some children's bodies will just naturally come closer than others' to the professional or adult aesthetic of how a dancer should look. If this happens spontaneously, that's fine. But most children express themselves physically in ways that adults don't recognize as "correct" according to the examples they've seen in theatrical dancing. A child actually has a range of physical expression that's lost at a certain level of maturity and sophistication. To sum it up, you can't expect to judge a child's progress in dance by adult aesthetic standards.

Adult models also may cause children to arrive at a dance studio hot for competition. But for children to retain their uniqueness, rivalry in the dance class should be played down. Whether

Janey does a step better than Ginny doesn't matter—just that each feels accomplishment and enjoyment in herself as an individual.

There are many tricks you can do in dancing: turns, splits, balances, high kicks, jumps. It's okay to try them, and some kids can do them pretty well. But dancing is about many more things than acrobatic feats, and to learn about quality, movement, and expressiveness in dance, you can't concentrate on tricks. How high children under the age of ten can kick and whether they can split has relatively little to do with the present or future relationship they might have to dancing.

Of course, the best trick of them all for little girls is standing on your toes. It happens to be extremely dangerous for kids under ten. No child under that age should put on a pair of pointe shoes, and never until she's had two or three years of regular, sound ballet training. Although dancing on pointe looks like it might be something apart from dancing in soft ballet shoes, it is in fact a natural extension of the ballet exercises that you do in soft shoes. These exercises make the back, hips, legs, and feet strong enough and develop body alignment correctly enough so that pointe work is possible.

Putting a child under ten or eleven on pointe can make her leg muscles bunchy, deform the very soft bones of her feet, and do irreparable damage to her knee cartilage and lower back. There's plenty of time to go on pointe after the age of eleven and still be a star. Margot Fonteyn started at twelve, and for one whole year, aside from her regular practice, did only simple exercises on pointe for five or ten minutes a day.

Boys. The taboo against dancing for boys centers on the question of sexual orientation. A popular misconception in America is that dance is for two kinds of kids: (1) girls; and (2) boys who are sissies or who will grow up to be homosexuals. "Boys who are boys" are supposed to be interested in athletics and competitive games. Actually, though, all children are interested in learning to use their bodies, and dance offers this opportunity in a particularly apt way for them, whether they're boys or girls.

Dancing for little boys has to be different from dancing for little girls, because boys' strength, coordination, and energy levels are different. They need some special types of movement to account for these, and a good teacher will usually incorporate some bigger, stronger dancing into a class when boys are present. The girls will do the movement, too, but the boys will get special benefit from it.

According to some, "It's becoming okay in America for boys to dance."[4] I hope the trend continues.

Early dance training as a bridge. The dance training a child under the age of eight or ten receives can be the preparation for a more formal discipline such as ballet. Strength, coordination, rhythm, a sense of physicality, control of the body, and the overall ability to follow movement patterns can be effectively taught, and will form the basis for further training in a more highly structured context. Early dance training shouldn't be merely amusing for kids, but rather should be thought of as a purposeful activity that brings them joyful development and may lay the groundwork for a more mature interest in dance.

Finding a class for children under ten. You can use the same research techniques for finding children's classes as you would for other types of classes. Look for ads or listings and keep your ears open for classes called "Movement Foundations for Children," "Dance Basics for Children," "Creative Rhythmic Movement," "Children's Modern Dance," "Creative Movement for Children," or "Pre-Ballet for Children." In some cases a class that's called "Ballet for Children" and that's given for kids under eight won't really be a ballet class, in which case it may be okay. If it does make an attempt at a traditional ballet format, it's not likely to be a good choice.

Tap is also offered for children under eight. Kids can learn a certain amount about rhythm from it, but the coordination of many steps in tap is far beyond their muscular grasp. As always, of course, there are exceptions. I would say, however, that a child under eight should have a broader dance experience than tap alone.

A child should attend class regularly once a week, except for summer vacations and other school holidays, when it's okay to skip them. In looking for a class, it's a good idea to seek one that is convenient in location and time. This will make it easier for a parent to deliver the child to class on a regular basis.

Evaluating classes for children under ten. One of your first steps in evaluating a class for children is to investigate the teacher's background thoroughly. Look for experience with children and a range of dance activities. A teacher who has studied or performed several types of dance usually will have a much wider base of operations when it comes to developing imaginative movement material for the children. It helps, too, if the teacher knows something about folk dancing.

Observing and evaluating the class, either before the child starts or during the first two or three classes, is essential if the child is going to avoid physical harm and learn anything useful. Below are listed the features to look for when observing. Of course, the greater the number of positive features you find, the better, but it's likely you won't find them all in any one class. I would say the three essentials are that the teacher have good rapport with the kids; that the children enjoy the class; and that the class be constructive for them. With these general ideas in mind, here are the specifics to look for:

- *The teacher's personality:* Does the teacher appeal to the children? seem to have a sense of play and involvement? seem to like teaching? Is the teacher energetic and spontaneous? warm and encouraging? Does the teacher show respect for the children and avoid belittling them? (By the way, the teacher need not look like a *dancer*; what's important is that the kids respond to the *person* that the teacher is.)
- *Variety:* Is there variety in the content of the class?

Do the children do such things as experiment with body weight—let it drop, lift it, catch it when it goes off balance, jump? Are body shapes and floor patterns explored—rounded and angular, straight, circular, serpentine, zigzag? Do the children do runs, hops, skips, leaps? Do they twist and bend their bodies? Does the teacher use exciting language—action words like *pounce, dart, freeze, grip, collapse, sink, whip, stamp, explode?* Does the teacher have the children use their voices? Do they do smooth and accented movement, fast and slow movement?

- *Play, attention, and discipline:* Is the teacher flexible in approach, using spontaneous events in the class as material to build into the lesson? Do you sense a give-and-take between the teacher and the kids? Or does the teacher concentrate heavily on discipline, seeming to follow a rigid lesson plan no matter what? Do you sense that the teacher becomes irritated when the kids don't behave? Are there frequent reprimands to pay attention? (There might be a need to remind the kids some of the time, but it shouldn't turn into a constant harangue, and the teacher should be good-natured and patient enough to put up with some mischief.) Do the children look involved in what they're doing, or do they seem frustrated or bored?

- *Accomplishment:* Does the teacher set goals for the children or help them set their own and then work with them toward achievement? Or are things kind of laissez-faire, with the kids running around being "butterflies" and "bees" with no particular place to land? Do the children look as if they are being challenged within reason? Do they seem to be sensing achievement?

- *Energy and motion:* Does the teacher often talk at

length while the kids have to sit or stand still? Or is there usually movement and a generally high energy expenditure? (Some movement should be quieter, some more vigorous; the kids might even be "statues," because that means they're putting imaginative energy into control of their bodies. But to require arbitrary sitting or standing still in order to listen to the teacher talk isn't really appropriate for young children, and especially not in dance class.)

- *Coordination and strength:* Do the children seem to be approaching the mastery of specific exercises that require coordination? strength? Is there enough repetition for them to work on mastering these skills? Or does the teacher seem to push too hard for or brush too lightly over things that really are beyond them? For example, are corrections made about coordination which is basically beyond the children's abilities because of their age? Do the children seem to be struggling against impossible odds?

- *Rhythm:* Does the teacher give special exercises or activities like clapping or swaying that involve the children specifically in identifying pulses or beats? Do the rhythmic exercises or activities seem to be almost within the children's grasp? Are rhythms also varied and integrated well throughout the lesson? Does the music or accompaniment sound fresh and vital?

- *Creativity and sociability:* Do the children get a chance to make up their own dances? Does the teacher encourage and guide them by imaginative suggestions such as: "Try a pretty dance. An angry dance. Who are the racing cars? The lumbering buses?"? Do the children work in pairs and groups as well as by themselves?

- *Adult values and tricks:* Does the teacher allow room for individual expression and variation? Or is there strict emphasis on one right way to do things? Does it look as if the kids are being asked to do tricks but not quite making it? Does the teacher make a point of pitting one student against another? Are the children pushed to "perform" in an embarrassing or exploitative way? Do you see any girls under the age of ten or eleven on pointe? (If you do, take your child out of the studio immediately.)

- *Boys:* Are large, powerful movements part of the lesson? Is there another boy or two in the class? (This usually makes a boy feel more comfortable.)
- *The bridge:* If you can possibly observe two different levels of classes taught at the school, look for a higher level of skill among the older or more advanced children. Can they do things the younger or beginning class can't? Can they do some of the same things better?
- *Other general features:* Does the teacher explain what the children are to do simply and clearly, with the result that there's minimal confusion when an exercise or activity starts? What do the children say about the class? What do the parents say? Are the facilities bright and cheerful?

Once a child has begun classes, a parent should observe from time to time to see whether the class continues to be suitable. Some schools have high turnover among their teaching staff, with the result that the class changes radically from one week to the next. There is also the chance that the class might turn out not to be the right one after all for the particular needs of a specific child.

One final word of caution: Beware of recital madness. Try to choose a class or school that doesn't focus all its attention on the Christmas or spring show. The recital-bent environment pushes kids toward a *product*, shortchanging them on the *process* that learning to dance is. Be sure the class is not so totally committed to performing *for others* that it eliminates any chance the children might have to dance in their own expressive way *for themselves*.

CHILDREN OVER EIGHT TO TEN

Around the age of ten—a bit younger for some and older for others—children are ready to begin a more formal study of dance technique. They might begin taking two classes a week at this age, although one a week may be better, depending on the child's available energy and time.

Selecting a type of dance. Parents often wonder whether they should choose one type of dance over another when children are so young. To take account of this question, in many schools a "smörgåsbord" class is taught that crams ballet, modern, jazz, acrobatic, and tap in various combinations into a one-hour class. Game as they are, children will pick up a lot from these classes; but, realistically speaking, there's more to be gained by concentrating on one in any given hour-long class. Which it will be in any one class should depend on the child's interests and abilities, and not purely on the parents' preferences. Many authorities on dance for children have ideas about what's good for kids, and you might want to take these into consideration, too.

For instance, there is support for the idea that it's advantageous to give kids the opportunity to create their own dances. Many modern dance classes and some jazz classes incorporate this creative element, integrating the building of technical skill and rhythmic awareness with a chance for the children to express themselves in their own dances. In ballet classes, however, this element is missing, and it's not often found in tap, either. Of course, a child can take two classes a week (time and budget permitting)—one in modern or jazz that has a creative part, and one in ballet or tap. It's an especially good idea to complement tap with one of the other types of dance, whether they have a creative element or not, because when tap is taken by itself it doesn't offer as broad a range of muscle activity as most kids need.

Acrobatic dance isn't really looked on as dance, although it's frequently taught at dancing schools. It teaches kids feats more than it teaches them about dancing, but there's no harm in a child's studying it. To broaden his or her experience to incorporate dance as an art form, a weekly ballet, modern, or jazz class can be added.

Parents often think in terms of a professional career for their children when they enroll them in a dance school. You do have to begin thinking about professional ballet dancing at an early age. Although I personally know exceptions to the rule (dancers who started training for ballet at eighteen or older), according to George Balanchine, if serious training isn't begun early enough—between ages eight and fifteen—becoming a fine ballet dancer is either extremely difficult or totally out of the question. There's some leeway for men (and they are the exceptions I know of) simply because there has traditionally been a scarcity of them. But that may be changing as more young boys become interested in dance.

Committing a child to the exacting study of ballet at the age of eight or nine, or even ten or twelve, has its disadvantages in the view of many teachers. Ernestine Stodelle, a former member of the Doris Humphrey company who has taught children for decades, reflected on her observation of a ballet class:

> Looking at the little girls who were . . . first and second year pupils, I thought that their painstaking efforts would certainly be rewarded should they decide in the far future to pursue the ballet as a vocation. But should they become business women, college graduates with other professional aims or "just marry" . . . then one wonders if the strain of meeting the demands of so exacting an art is to be recommended for such young children. Even when pedagogical standards are highest . . . development at this stage means an accumulation of details rather than a deepening knowledge of dance itself.[5]

Nonetheless, ballet is still the choice of many children and their parents, either because it meets their aesthetic preferences or because they're aiming toward a professional ballet career. Once a decision is made to head in this direction, ballet classes should be quite frequent: twice a week in the first year of study, three times in the second, and so on. Friends, free time, and family and social life will fall by the wayside as practice intensifies. Some things to consider are: Does the child really have enough time and energy for it? Will the parents be able to afford a long period of paying for classes and dance gear? Can a start-stop-start-again situation be avoided so that the child will have continuous training? And, finally, can a child under fifteen cope with making a decision that will so drastically affect his or her life-style? Obviously enough have; the exquisite ballet dancers we see today are evidence. But for many children and their parents, it's not an easy choice to make.

One of the realities to be confronted is that a child of twelve or thirteen hasn't yet reached full physical, mental, or emotional maturity, and after several years of study it may turn out that he or she isn't suited physically or temperamentally for a career in ballet. Although the experience of training isn't really a waste, the disappointment can be serious.

Kids should experiment, and parents should guide and help evaluate what's best. Reading about dance may help make decisions, or at least give a better understanding of what's involved.[6] Consider, as well, that a summer dance camp or summer study in a place like Jacob's Pillow can make the experimentation and the resulting conclusion more realistic.

Pressing for a premature decision about a professional career isn't necessary, of course. Children can still dance for the sake of dancing without its consuming the major part of their lives. If they get a solid movement foundation and are taught to work intelligently on strength, stretch, and coordination, there's no reason why they can't decide to enter the profession at a later age in a capacity other than ballet superstar.

Incidentally, if a child aims toward becoming a professional dancer, it will take time. Trying to speed up the process usually won't work. For example, at-home practice without the watchful eye of a teacher doesn't usually pay off very much in comparison to the toll it takes on the child's free time. In some cases the child runs the risk of practicing bad habits. It's best for parents to encourage, guide, and be patient, and not to push.

Finding and evluating a class for children over eight or ten. Word-of-mouth, ads, and telephone listings will work here again, and the teacher's background should be looked into as well. For profession-bound students, check the teacher's background for performing experience and for a record of whom he or she has trained (any dancers you've seen and liked?). Also try the alternative of identifying dancers you and the child admire and looking into their background to see who has trained them. Or find the school that's affiliated with any professional company you think the child might head toward and learn about its programs for identifying and training talented youngsters.

Observation and careful evaluation of classes are in order, of course. You can apply the same standards for evaluating classes in this age group as were recommended for younger children, with these differences:

- *Discipline:* The teacher can ask for a bit more discipline from the kids and allow a bit less play (though still being agreeable about it).
- *Imaginative suggestions:* These should suit the more-mature interests of older children.
- *Technique:* When the children work intently on any purely technical aspects of dance, their bodies should never look distorted, twisted, or misaligned. (See the evaluation notes in the first chapter.) If ballet technique is taught, creative elements won't be present in the class, but instead the traditional ballet class sequence of warm-up, center work, and across-the-floor combinations should be followed.

Adults

The first time I wore a pair of pointe shoes, I was a full-grown adult of twenty-three. Somehow I had missed out on dancing as a child. My mother had taken me to a storefront dancing school for a few months when I was about seven. I'm not sure exactly what we did there, but I do remember how much I loved putting on my light blue tunic for class and how sorry I was when I outgrew it. I think the school closed after a while, or else there was some other reason I never went back. In any case, dance classes didn't work out after that first brief encounter.

While I was in college, I discovered folk dancing, which I did endlessly even as my grades fell. I also took a semester of modern dance. Again, though, of all the experiences in this class, a costume stands out most vividly: the teacher's calf-length modern dance skirt. I remember that I didn't find it as appealing as my light blue tunic, however, and never bothered to buy one for myself. After that semester I found I had taken the only modern dance class that was offered, and it didn't seem that interesting to repeat the same thing for another semester.

Even though I didn't study dance formally until after I was out of college, it always held a fascination for me, as I think it does for many people who reach adulthood never having fully explored the experience. School, family obligations, social life, career goals, other people's expectations of you, or simply a lack of exposure or availability of classes prevent you from getting involved. You might keep telling yourself you'll take classes one day, but before you know it you're in your twenties or installed in a career. By then you think, Well, it must be too late for dancing.

At some point you become aware of the importance of physical fitness for total health, and depending on the structure of your life, you manage to squeeze in a little exercise: a workout at the gym, jogging, tennis, squash, swimming, or maybe the

Royal Canadian Air Force exercises. If you're simply too busy to do anything organized, you might count on the running around you do to keep you in shape.

But as you're yawning your way through another sit-up, or having trouble getting into last year's summer slacks, you might ask yourself, as I did: Why not try dancing? What did I do in that little blue tunic, in reality a rather plain and ordinary garment, that made it so fascinating? Why did I folk-dance at school to the extent that I nearly flunked out? Is dancing really so different from exercising or jogging as people say it is?

Just as I decided to satisfy my curiosity, you might also, and find yourself ready to sign up for a class. Here's what you should think about as you do.

GENERAL PHYSICAL CONDITION

The age at which you begin dance classes isn't any hindrance if your general physical condition is good. If you've been active in sports (other than golf) for most of your life, and have remained strong and flexible, your age won't necessarily be that much of a problem, even if you're past forty. The older you are, though, the harder it will be for you if you're not in good physical condition. A twenty-year-old won't require as much time or effort to get back into shape as a thirty- or forty-year-old person will.

If you are over forty and not in great shape, it's also a good idea to have a medical checkup before you begin any exercise program, dancing included.

MIND-BODY CONNECTION

The more you engage in physical activity, the stronger the link between your head and your muscles. Unfortunately, the reverse is also true: The less active you are, the weaker the link.

If you've done things that require the coordination of the larger muscles in your body (those controlling your legs and torso, for example, as opposed to those controlling your fingers), then you're likely to have a basis for building some dance skills. A quick isolation test should tell you how in touch your mind and muscles are: Stand up and try to move your rib cage from side to side without moving your hips beneath it. Now try moving it forward and back without moving your hips. If you can do this fairly quickly and easily, without having to ponder and make a long series of false starts, the connection is likely to be in good shape. If you can't, though, all is not lost; you'll just have to work a little harder to find it again.

INTELLECTUAL MATURITY

One big thing you have going for you when you're older is your more mature intellect. You're capable of thinking and analyzing a lot more than a youngster is, and while this won't necessarily replace the practice you'll have to do to acquire skill, it can make it more productive. You can use your head to be more efficient and decisive. Being older, you'll know more about who you are and what you want, and you can be more directed and practical in going after your goals.

DANCE AND CHANGE AS REJUVENATORS

Recently I read an article about a man, Dr. Hideo Hokawa of Japan, who began studying ballet at the age of sixty-four, dancing the role of Count Montague in Prokofiev's *Romeo and Juliet* after he'd studied awhile. Dr. Hokawa says that constantly changing his interests is the secret of his adeptness, and he has in fact gone through and continues to be intently occupied by activities in aeronautics, medicine, rocketry, music, and sports.

The man is without question a phenomenon. But I think his basic concept of change as a means of keeping yourself versatile, flexible, and young is a fundamental truth. By varying your interests, and pursuing each with wholehearted commitment and enthusiasm, you confront the kind of mental and physical challenges that are revitalizing.

SELECTING A TYPE OF DANCE

Modern dance is a good choice for beginning adults, particularly Hawkins technique or any other eclectic kind of modern class that involves stretching and big body movement. Jazz is an excellent choice also. Both modern and jazz have you working on stretch, strength, and coordination of the large muscles of your body without bogging you down in extensive and detailed technical analysis.

Ballet is okay for many beginning adults up until their late twenties. At that point, it's better to start in jazz or modern, which aren't so exacting in such a stylized way. If you start ballet in your early twenties *and* you have a strong, flexible, well-coordinated body *and* you study conscientiously, you can develop quite a good technique.

Many beginning adults also prefer modern classes to ballet because in modern dance you can make more use of what you already know about moving. Natural movements like walking, running, and leaping are part of most modern dance classes. This makes them initially easier to grasp than ballet. You'll still develop strength, stretch, and coordination as you would in ballet; it will just be in a different context.

Tap for adult beginners is fine, so long as it fits your basic coordination ability and provided you're not too concerned about building flexibility. If you want to both tap and stretch, you can supplement your tap classes with jazz, ballet, or modern.

FINDING CLASSES

To give adult beginners the special attention and pacing they need, more and more schools and teachers are offering classes explicitly for them. These are often called something like "Adult Fundamentals," "Adult Ballet," or "Movement Basics for Adults."

You should follow the same research techniques as were suggested in Chapter 1 for finding a likely place to take classes.

Then, of course, your next step is to evaluate the class to see if it's the right one for you.

EVALUATING CLASSES

All the guidelines in Chapter 1 for observing and taking classes are good ones to apply. Also add the following:

☆ *Does the teacher generally work carefully and slowly with students, particularly when stretching exercises are done?* If you're around forty and haven't done much physically all your life, you can injure yourself if you do too much too vigorously or forcefully, too soon.

☆ *Does the teacher demonstrate exercises so that they seem within reasonable reach of the students?* A young or very agile teacher will sometimes demonstrate an exercise to an older group of students, showing strength and flexibility that are in outer space compared to the students' capabilities. Demonstrations of exercises should look like something the students might be able to tackle.

☆ *Is loosening and lengthening stressed throughout the class?* Since most adult beginners are confronted with problems of inflexible muscles and somewhat frozen joints, there should be strong emphasis on loosening up.

☆ *Is the teacher exceptionally encouraging and patient?* There is a long road ahead to fitness for many adults, and they need all the encouragement and patience they can get.

— *Does the teacher give frequent technical or detailed corrections that are beyond the students' abilities to understand or apply?* Again, goals should be realistic. It's more important for beginning adults to move than it is for them to worry about the finer points.

— *Does the teacher explain the purpose of exercises?* Much can be accomplished by putting the adult's more mature intellect to work. You should hear reasons for the exercises in the form of instructions like "You're stretching the backs of your legs now; feel the length back there." "This exercise is to strengthen the muscles in your abdomen."

— *Do students experience a good workout?* While the teacher shouldn't push too hard, the exercises should be vigorous enough so that students can become more than just superficially involved. If strength, stretch, and coordination are to develop and the head-body connection made, work has to be done.

SPECIAL NOTES FOR ADULT BEGINNERS WHO ARE REALLY OUT OF SHAPE

If you've gone through most of your life with minimal exercise and find yourself seriously out of condition as you begin dance classes, there are some special things you should keep in mind until you begin to firm and loosen up. These will protect you from injury and make the experience of class more enjoyable:

(1) Find a class where you can work very, very slowly at first. Don't do anything with suddenness. Use the time both to exercise and to concentrate on becoming attuned to bodily sensations.

(2) Try to keep up with the class, but if you know it's feeling like too much for you, stop. Get physically involved but don't overexert yourself.

(3) Follow the teacher's instructions as closely as you can. You may find that nothing will feel natural or right to you for a long while, and it may make you want to fall back into familiar habits. Try not to. Really listen to what the teacher says and do your best to apply it to your work in class.

Age Anxiety

I started lying about my age the minute I decided to make dancing my profession. It was something all the dancers I knew did on their résumés. To admit to being more than a reasonably young age was to jeopardize your career. In the dance world, and in America generally, it's supposed to be better to be younger. The fewer years you have chalked up against you, the more valuable a commodity you are.

Admittedly, your body changes as you get older. Admittedly, as a dancer you're dependent on your body, and some of the changes it goes through may not be particularly helpful to your dancing. But it doesn't help your dancing to worry about it, deny it, or become obsessed with it, either. The more you focus on age as a negative factor in your life, the more it will become so.

You can look at your maturity in constructive ways. Your chronological age doesn't necessarily correlate with your body's suitability for dance. Many people have "young" bodies—flexible and resilient physiques—throughout their lives. Erik Bruhn throws positive light on the subject, too. When he was interviewed during one of PBS's "Dance in America" programs, he said that as you get older, you can still dance the younger roles in the classical ballets. Your insight into them sharpens, and as a result your performance becomes that much more powerful. When you're older you have greater wisdom and experience to draw on, which can enable you to more adeptly round the edges and fill the phrases of your dancing. You can still maintain or improve your technique as you mature, but the best part is developing your ability to comprehend and feel what dancing is about.

It's also constructive to know that there are alternatives—that if your age works against you in one situation, you don't have to pack up and quit. For example, if you don't start dancing early enough to become a premier danseur or a prima ballerina, you may be able to have a performing career in modern dance. Or, if your heart is set on ballet, you may want to work toward performing with a smaller professional company or a community group. Or you don't have to work toward performing at all. You can simply take classes and dance because it's something you love to do.

Try never to make the assumption that you're too old for something you really want to do until you've given yourself a fair chance. Your desire and motivation can mean ten times as much as your age in enabling you to reach your goals. And don't listen to the spoilsports along the way who talk about age as though it's some kind of disease. It is rather a simple fact that should be treated in proportion to the real part it plays in your life. Keep it in perspective and in its place, and it really shouldn't present any problems.

3

Especially for Beginners: Thoughts and Suggestions to Get You Off to a Good Start

Beginners at anything are in a very special place. They often have an openness and an innocence that are true assets to their first efforts. I believe in that phenomenon known as beginner's luck, whether it be in games of chance or in dance. This is not to say that taking dance class is like rolling dice, just that as a beginner you're not at a disadvantage. In fact, you're probably in a much better place than you think.

Your reasons for starting to dance may range from curiosity about dance as an art form to the grand opening of a new career, and your physical attributes may facilitate your opening moves or they may present obstacles to be overcome. The notes that follow describe experiences that I and people I know have had when beginning to dance. Depending on your background and assets, some will be exactly like the experiences you'll have; others won't. You'll also find some suggestions that I think will get you off to a good start, no matter what your attributes.

You'll notice as you read through the rest of this book that some of the topics I've introduced in this chapter appear again in an expanded form. I've broken them out here because I think they're particularly important for beginners to concentrate on and so that you'll have more than one chance to think about them. Don't worry about having to understand everything in this chapter all at once.

Stretch

Most beginners have some problem with flexibility. You may not be able to touch your toes or, when sitting, to stretch your legs out to anything more than an unhappily narrow V. You may feel at times that you have rusty springs for hips. And to top it all off, you'll always be left gawking at someone in class who is smugly placing nose to knee, chatting comfortably in a split, or cracking gum casually with foot in hand extended overhead.

A battle with tightness can be discouraging, especially in the face of your rubber-jointed fellow students. The best way to handle it is to relax. Stretch comes only when you're able to let go of the right muscles sufficiently to allow them to lengthen. As you learn to relax and they grow accustomed to being stretched, they'll fight you less when you next ask them to extend themselves.

Muscles must always be warm when they are being stretched. Although you will see students stretching before class (when they may not be warmed up), for most beginners it's better to stretch after class or simply to do stretching exercises at the times when the teacher builds them into the class.

Muscles and the tendons that connect them to bone are together designed to stretch to about one and a half times their resting length. Ligaments, which are strong, fibrous bands that hold the bones of joints together, are not as stretchable as muscles, but can be cajoled into giving a bit. The younger you are when you start the stretching process, the easier it is and the more stretch you'll be able to develop. But you can still loosen up quite a bit all the way into adulthood.

In addition to stretching in your regular dance classes, you may want to try a special "stretch class." Here you'll spend the entire time working on loosening and lengthening your body. Stretch classes can help a great deal; however, I recommend them only after you've been dancing regularly for six months to a year. Before that time you may not have enough familiarity with your internal body cues to understand what's happening and to protect yourself against pulling or tearing a muscle.

Whenever you're stretching, some important things to remember are: (1) be warmed up; (2) don't hold your breath; (3) avoid stretching too strenuously or too vigorously (for example, if you do bounces to stretch, they should be light, easy bounces rather than big, forceful ones; or use just the weight of your torso without any push behind it to stretch out your back and the backs of your thighs); (4) keep thinking long and loose in your head.

Stretching is sometimes painful because of the body's natural defense mechanisms. Muscles are equipped with sensing devices that sound an alarm when they're being stretched beyond a certain point. This is to protect them against possible tearing. The alarm is received in your central nervous system, and it sets up an unconscious reaction which causes the muscle to contract instead of to relax and stretch. You're left trying to stretch a muscle that's determined to contract. This phenomenon is known as the "stretch reflex." You have a better chance of sneaking around the stretch reflex and avoiding the alarm if your muscles are warm, and if you relax, keep breathing, think loose, and don't push too hard.

Strength and Coordination

Strength and coordination, like flexibility, are a combination of what you're born with and what you develop through work. Which muscles you need to develop and how they are used will depend on the type of dance you study. But in general, any strenuous physical activity that you haven't engaged in regularly will cause you at first to use muscles you aren't accustomed to using, and will call upon the coordination of your muscle groups in new ways. With regular repetition, your muscles will strengthen and you'll stop feeling as though you have three legs and five arms to control. You'll need to be patient while this is happening and to avoid overdoing it or becoming frustrated. The clearer and calmer you can keep your approach to acquiring strength and coordination, the better off you'll be.

Placement

Placement is the alignment of body parts and the resulting distribution of weight through the feet to the floor (for example, head centered over the spine, rib cage directly over the pelvis, legs descending properly from the hip sockets, weight over the toes). When a dancer is correctly "placed," less muscle is needed to perform movement because the weight of body parts does not resist it but instead actually helps it. Coordination is easier too, because no extra muscles are used trying to hold body parts, thus freeing them to participate in coordinated movement. A dancer works to achieve correct placement throughout his or her dancing life because it is the way to attain fluidity of movement and excellence of technique.

From your very first dance class you'll be working toward good placement, and while you'll also be working to develop stretch, strength, and coordination, keep in mind that placement is a partner to them. Don't assume it's all done through brute force. Strength, stretch, and placement play reciprocal roles and also affect coordination. Of course, you'll develop above average stretch and strength once you're beyond a certain level in dance. But even then good placement allows you to use your stronger, longer muscles more efficiently.

In class you'll usually be given help in placement by the teacher. He or she will have you do such things as raise or lower your chin, align your pelvis so that it doesn't tip forward or backward, and get your body weight off your heels and more evenly distributed across the soles of your feet. Your job will be to try to sense the difference between your usual habits of placement and those the teacher is trying to encourage in you. You may at first feel as though your nose is about to make contact with the floor, but once you notice you're standing, try to become familiar with your new placement and how your muscles feel when working in it.

Movement and Music

There's a great deal of detail in dancing—many different parts of your body to move, directions to move them in, dynamics to use, rhythms to follow, phrases to recognize. When you're just beginning, all these details can present a staggering amount to learn. It's important to remember, though, that dancing is movement, and not just details about movement. As a beginner, try not to worry so much about performing every last minute item absolutely correctly. Instead, try to build your sense of movement. For example, you may not hold your arm and hand in precisely the shape or position they're supposed to be in, but if you manage to sense that you or a part of you has traveled through space and you recognize the physicality of it, you will have come much closer to dancing than if you had used all your attention to worry about your arm.

You can sense movement and dancing in any exercise you do in class. A simple tendu, for instance (in which all you do is slide your foot along the floor to a pointed position), is an opportunity to sense the height of your torso and the length of your leg as they participate together in making the change from one shape in space to another. It is an opportunity to experience dancing, and not just an exercise in which you concentrate on whether you've kept your foot on the floor long enough or pointed your foot strongly enough. You'll be concerned about those aspects of the exercise too, but don't lose sight of the fact that you are in motion. Always try to keep this sense of dancing with you. It will help you immensely as a beginner, and it will be vital to you as you go on in your studies.

Music can be especially useful in giving you a sense of movement. One of the prominent thoughts in your mind as you begin classes should be to listen carefully to the music played and to follow it in meter and in spirit as best you can. Music is a great organizer for movement and can integrate all the smaller details of dancing so that they don't seem so overpowering. All you need to do is to listen and let it flow through your body.

At-Home Practice

It's not necessary and it can be damaging when you're just beginning if you attempt to do dance exercises outside of class. Unless your teacher has suggested and carefully demonstrated exercises for you to do at home, don't bother. Don't try to devise your own or do the standard sit-ups, leg lifts, and so on. Until you become more familiar with techniques of working your body, you can do yourself more harm than good. Furthermore, research has shown that the best way to develop strength and coordination of muscles that are to be used for a specific activity is to do the activity itself. There are ways of breaking physical activity down into component parts and practicing the parts separately. As a beginner, however, you may do this incorrectly. Check with your teacher before you embark on any exercises you think may help your dancing, and in general, until you reach a more advanced level, expect to lay the groundwork for your dance technique during the time you spend in class.

Soreness and Stiffness

If you have to climb up or descend any stairs after your first few dance classes, you may feel as though you're going through torture from the Dark Ages. The muscles in your thighs and calves may be particularly sore, especially the day or two after class. The soreness and stiffness most beginners feel after a strenuous dance class are just temporary conditions of the muscles. (Incidentally, even seasoned professionals get stiff and sore muscles when they return to class after more than five days without exercise.) You can ease your discomfort by soaking in a hot tub immediately after you return home from class. Actually, you won't feel any discomfort until the next day, but the best time to soak is before this happens. Massage will also relieve the condition, as it helps bring a supply of blood to the muscles, thereby speeding the recovery process. And don't let stiffness and soreness keep you away from class. You can actually work some of it out by using the muscles, because exercise also increases the supply of blood to them.

If the soreness doesn't go away after a few days, you may have strained or pulled a muscle, in which case you may need to go easy on that area of your body in class or take a few days off for total rest. After a while you'll understand your body's messages and be able to tell soreness and stiffness from a strain or a pulled muscle.

Self-consciousness

If having someone watch you makes you freeze, blush, and become riveted to the spot, you may run into some feelings of self-consciousness during your first few weeks or months of dance class. You won't be helped either by the fact that you're probably not in the habit of cavorting about clad in skin-hugging garments that show your every sinew. No matter how great you look in them, you may still feel conspicuous and awkward. Of course, that feeling passes once you steep yourself in the dancing. Some things that might help while you're agonizing through this stage are: (1) Concentrate on what you're feeling inside your body, not how you may look from the outside; (2) keep breathing; (3) remember that almost everybody feels or has felt exactly as you feel now, and that the uneasiness disappears in time.

Attention Factors

Another demon of the beginner's route is trying to remember the exercises the teacher wants you to do. Even a maddeningly simple series of steps, demonstrated for you twice and carefully explained by the teacher, will slip impishly out of your head as soon as you try to make your first move. Take heart and don't enroll in any five-day memory-improvement courses. You'll see the same steps over and over again, so eventually they'll sink in. It takes a different kind of visual and mental attention to look at a dance combination and remember it. Developing that attention is just part of the bag of tricks you'll learn.

Your auditory attention will also be pressed into unusual service. Of course you're used to listening and trying to understand what people say to you. But sometimes trying to understand what's being said in dance class is like trying to follow driving directions when there aren't any street signs—at least until you're familiar with the inner territory of your body and begin to post the signs for yourself. You'll be on the most direct route to this end if you open your attention out as fully as you can and try to do exactly what the teacher is asking. Try not to sink into what you know is comfortable, but rather be prepared to go uncompromisingly ahead. You may feel strange at first, but soon things will start clicking and you'll be on friendly if not familiar terms with the workings of your body. The teacher's directions will baffle you less and less as you discover the corresponding inner clues your body has to offer.

Sweating

I never knew how much perspiration I was capable of producing until I started dancing. When you're not used to it, it can be quite a shock and something of a nuisance.

The amount you'll sweat in class depends for one thing on your basic anatomy and physiology. Some people just have more sweat glands that produce greater quantities of perspiration. Sweating is also related to how efficiently you've learned to use your muscles. When you're just beginning you may use many more than you really need to, and as a result you'll generate more of the body heat that's the cause of your perspiring. Breathing also plays a part in it. If you hold your breath you're likely to sweat more than if you breathe as fully as you can.

Unless you're born programmed for minimal perspiring, you're likely to sweat in dance classes. You can take a small towel with you into the studio if it makes you feel better to wipe off every once in a while. And you'll probably want to keep your hair off your face and neck. You can use cologne, aftershave lotion, talc, or any other item or device that makes you feel better about sweating. Try not to think of sweat as something distasteful, though. It's really only your body's way of trying to cool you down.

Muscle Cramps

Muscles in your calves and feet are particularly susceptible to cramping when you're just beginning to study dance. A cramp is a persistent contraction of a muscle (or group of muscles) beyond the time you voluntarily want it to contract. Although muscle cramps don't mean you've injured yourself, they're quite painful and you'll find you want to relieve them promptly.

A good way to handle a cramp in your calf is to sit on the floor, bend your knee, and put the sole of your foot on the floor. Then use the heels of your hands to massage and jiggle your calf until the cramp goes.

For a foot cramp, sit on the floor and take your foot in both hands, making it as limp as you can. Knead your entire foot as though it were dough.

It may take a minute or two to coax a cramp into leaving, but don't panic. A cramp may be a bit startling because it comes on suddenly and is acutely painful, but it usually disappears quite readily if you allow the muscle(s) involved to relax enough.

Occasionally a muscle cramp will return shortly after you've relieved it. If this happens repeatedly with the same muscle or muscle group, try to concentrate on not "grabbing" when you put your muscles to work. Think, instead, of easing into the position or movement you want to achieve. Your teacher may be able to help you do this and thereby to avoid cramps.

As you grow stronger and learn to use your muscles fluidly, cramps will just about disappear from your experiences in dance class.

Fatigue

Beginners classes are often just one hour long (many professional classes are a full two hours), but even stout-hearted fellows may start to tire as the minute hand nears the three-quarter mark. Many beginners look longingly toward chairs or little corner nooks at about this time, thinking, Just a short rest before I finish the class. Unless you are in serious physical distress and do not plan to continue the class (or the teacher has so instructed you), don't sit down. It's simply bad for your muscles. Even a four- or five-minute rest will cool them down to the point where you may injure yourself when you go back out onto the floor to do that last dance step. Dance classes are paced so that the movements you do toward the end are bigger and require warmer muscles than those you do at the beginning. Don't open yourself up to injury. If you feel too tired to continue, you should leave the class (with a polite nod to the teacher if you make eye contact). If fatigue hits you while you're waiting your turn to perform an exercise or step, try walking quietly to and fro at the back of the studio. You can also relieve fatigue by standing with your weight evenly distributed on both feet rather than dropping your weight into one hip or draping yourself over a barre.

Operating Procedures

As you take more classes, you'll develop stamina, and soon, instead of wanting to sit down before class is over, you'll want to stay afterward to work on a tricky combination or two. If there are no students rushing into the studio for the next class, this is a good time to ask one of the more advanced students in your class to work with you on the combination. (Intermediate and advanced-level dancers sometimes take a beginners class when they want to work more slowly and carefully.) It may be tempting to ask for this kind of help from fellow students during class, but in most cases it is distracting to the teacher and other students and can disrupt class flow. The teacher, unless running off to fulfill another commitment, will also usually work with you after class if you ask for help.

Being sensitive to the tenor of the class while meeting your own needs is part of studying dance productively. You'll pick up pointers as you go along, and Chapter 8 presents many more, but it may be hard to keep track of them all when you're just beginning because you have so many other things to learn. Three good general rules that will help you through until you learn the more specific ones are: (1) Try not to do things that disrupt the class; (2) command a space for yourself, but be respectful of the space others in class have etched out for themselves; (3) stay alert.

Class Frequency

How often should you take class when you're beginning? If you can work it into your schedule, you should plan to start with no fewer than two classes a week taken a few days apart— say on Mondays and Thursdays or Tuesdays and Fridays. This gives your body time to rest and recuperate between classes. If you can fit only one class into your busy schedule, you should try to take it on the same day each week. Generally your body likes to do things in a regular rhythm—eat, sleep, work, and so on. It will adjust more happily to the demands of dance if you put your request in for approximately the same time or times each week. As you advance, you should test out adding one class a week to your normal routine and see how it feels for a month or so.

Private Classes

A question that many motivated beginners ask is, Should I take private classes? Because you want to feel more progress than you think you're making, you may wonder if private classes will help you. Before you invest your money, here are a few things to consider.

Much of the learning of physical skills is based on (1) amount of repetition and (2) elapsed time. In other words, you have to do a step or an exercise over and over again before your muscles will catch on, and you can't cram all your practice into a short time. Strength and coordination grow as a function of how you space your practice and not only on the basis of the practice itself.

Watching other beginners and other dancers in class and noticing how the teacher corrects them will teach you a lot, too. You'll be missing out on this valuable learning opportunity if you're in a private class by yourself.

You also get energy from the people around you, and whereas in a group class you can depend on others when you're not at a high energy level, in a private class it'll be just you and the teacher.

If you're anxious to experiment with private classes, you should probably take them in conjunction with group classes so that you can get the benefits of both situations. Talk to other students you know who may have tried private classes and see what they have to say.

4

From Head to Toe:
Dressing
for Safety and Technique

This is the age of the costume. Even IBM's starchiest executives are reportedly flashing colored shirts from behind their gray flannel suits. Dressing for your job or a daily round of activities invites imagination and a sense of theater these days, and many of the people you see on the street make a marvelous feast for the eyes. Clothes are a grand way to unleash the inner you, and you should feel free to give full expression of yourself through your attire.

You need a slightly different approach for dance class, however, because there's literally more to it than meets the eye. Dressing for dance class must also meet the demands of safety and technique.

As an experienced dancer, you'll be familiar with many of the suggestions made here, but you may also discover some things you didn't know about (for example, the pros and cons of warm-up clothing for performers). Beginners are likely to find all of this information new and useful, and if you're somewhere in between, you'll undoubtedly run across a great deal that will be helpful.

Leotards and Tights

The basic dancer uniform is leotard and tights, but the dance-fashion craze has populated the stores with so many varieties and colors, you won't feel your personal style is cramped. Whatever their cut or hue, leotards and tights are designed to display the lines of your body clearly without having you go stark naked, and to make your body free for whatever movement is humanly possible. It's apparent why your body must be free for movement in dancing, but you should also be aware that in dressing for class it's important to have your body lines be plainly visible. There are two reasons: (1) so your teacher can see whether you're working correctly in class; and (2) to conform to the aesthetics of the many types of dance (ballet, modern, and jazz among them) which address the concept of the lines the human body makes in space.

In performance various kinds of costuming may alter the basic human figure, but especially in class you'll want to experience the traditional aesthetic base of such types of dance as ballet and modern, which is the uncluttered body line. There's a bit more flexibility in jazz classes, and tap focuses more on the timing of steps than on your body lines. Your dress options are therefore quite a bit wider in these contexts. But for freedom of movement, even in jazz and tap classes you may find that leotard and tights are the most practical arrangement.

If you're a male dancer, you may wear a close-fitting T-shirt instead of a leotard, and a belt or suspenders to hold your tights up. Beneath your tights, a dance belt, which is different from an ordinary athletic supporter or jockstrap, is a must. If you forget to take it to class with you, you should probably forget about taking class. You won't be very comfortable, and you might do yourself some damage.

With respect to supportive garments, you may run into a teacher who recommends a "dance girdle" for women. Unless you've just had a baby, there's no need for one. In fact, it's probably not a good idea at all, because it interferes with your awareness of the use and development of your abdominal muscles.

In some classes a teacher will recommend that you wear only a leotard and no tights. (This is true in Hawkins technique classes.) Supposedly you develop more feeling for the workings of your leg muscles that way. Some studio floors are not particularly warm or clean, however, and when you do floor exercises you may be uncomfortable without tights on. Until you've tried it you won't know whether you like it, but if you've elected a class in which it's recommended, you probably should experiment with your tights off. Then you can decide for yourself which you prefer.

Tights and leotards are manufactured in different fabric weights and with varying amounts of stretch. Quite often, the heavier the fabric, the less the stretch. Heavier material also retains more warmth—something you may or may not want, depending on the conditions under which you'll be dancing.

Depending on your body dimensions and taste, you'll find some leotards and tights more comfortable than others. Before you lay your hard-earned cash on the counter for them, be sure they fit well and especially that you can move easily in them. Stretch your arms and legs while you're trying them on; bend over from the waist and also do some side stretches with your arms up over your head. Lift your legs and try sitting down. Some brands of tights tend toward short legs, even when they're clearly labeled "long" or "tall." It doesn't help your dancing to have your legs bound together mid-thigh, so watch out for them if you tend toward long limbs.

In general, you'll find that when you're comfortable in your dance clothes and feel you look good in them, you dance better. Choose your dance attire with both eyes open: one on comfort and the other on appearance.

When leotards and tights get old and runny, unless you like random see-through rivulets and holes, sew them up or buy new ones. It doesn't bother some dancers, and it may not bother you, but a hole near the crotch in my tights always makes me a little reluctant about raising my legs. It inhibits me when I want to feel free and dancy. If you're the same way, resort to a needle and thread or the nearest dance-clothes store to pull your wardrobe together.

To keep your leotards and tights stretchy and preserve their elastic waists, they should ideally be washed in a very mild soap (like Ivory) and never put into a clothes dryer. If you have the time and patience to treat them so carefully, your dance clothes will look and fit better for a longer time. You also have to be realistic about your schedule, though. Buying new clothes more often may be simpler and make more sense than using your energies to do hand laundry.

Security and Warm-up Clothing

As any performer knows, putting on costume and make-up creates a special frame of mind and makes you more secure in the role you are about to play. Putting on your dance gear for class works in the same way. As dancers grow more deeply involved in the class routine, they often develop fondnesses for special pairs of tights or leotards and perhaps a close relationship with a security garment or two. Many dancers become almost addicted to items of clothing or other rituals to put them in a "class" frame of mind.

Of course, it's not all in the mind. Leg warmers, ankle warmers, knee warmers, and body warm-up suits made of lightweight wool or jersey do raise the temperature of the body parts they're covering and help the muscles and joints work better. They can be especially useful when you have an injury. Keeping an injured knee or ankle warm with a piece of wool covering helps the healing process. But remember that if you want corrections from the teacher on the very important issue of alignment, you have to allow enough of your natural body lines to show. Too much covering can distort and hide problems that your teacher could otherwise help you with. Some dancers dress for class in an awesome array of warmers, sweaters, socks, odd pieces of wool, scarves, and blousy rubber sweat pants. Luckily, their teachers are often adept at visually piercing the coverings, but that takes real looking. Unless you're keeping an injured part of your body warm, wear only the clothes you really need.

Bell-bottom pants, also called "jazz pants," are used either in place of tights or as warm-ups over them. I once saw a dancer wearing a pair who looked like a hobbled horse every time he tried to get one leg quickly out from behind the other. Bell bottoms may give a breezy look to loose, easy movement, but any voluminous fabric hanging around your ankles can trip you up when you least expect it and possibly cause a fall and injury. Use your judgment about the sensibleness of attire that creates bulk at your ankles. It can never look or feel so good that you'll want to sprain your ankle or break your leg for it. It has the additional disadvantage of hiding your ankles and feet from the teacher, who would otherwise be able to give you corrections concerning those areas of your body.

Rubber sweat pants became the rage a few years back, when they received rave notices as simultaneous warmers and spot reducers. They do warm you up; whether they reduce anything is unclear. But they also have been identified as the culprit in arthritis because they stimulate sweat while you're in motion but cool down immediately, turning the sweat into an ice bath, when you stop. If you opt for rubber sweat pants, wear woolen warmers under them; they will retain enough of your body heat to take the threat of arthritis out of the situation.

A close second to rubber sweat pants for some dancers is plastic wrap. They use it (usually underneath tights or leotards) on the parts of their body they want to reduce. Again, it's not clear that it helps, and it can present the same arthritis threat as sweat pants.

Watch out also for total dependence on warm-up garments. They're good aids to raising the internal temperature of your muscles and joints, but if you intend to perform, your muscles must be able to generate sufficient heat themselves, even if your costume consists only of a scanty tunic or a gold lamé dance belt. Be sure you maintain the ability to raise the internal temperature of your muscles and joints without lots of covering. One way to do this is to take off your warm-up garments piece by piece or layer by layer as you progress through class. If you never dance without your warm-up clothes on, you open yourself up to injury when you have to take it all off to perform. Also, don't leave your warm-up clothes on until the last possible second before you jump on stage. This shocks your muscles and, again, may lead to injury. Give your muscles several minutes to adjust to the environmental temperature and heat themselves up from the inside before you go out to do your number.

Some studios are cold in wintry climates, and warm-up garments throughout the whole class are in order in these places without question. Being too cold while dancing is not only uncomfortable, it can also be extremely dangerous. If your muscles and joints aren't warm enough when you ask them to take on the heavy load of strenuous dance movement, they'll react poorly. They won't want to accept the demands you're placing on them, and will object by sending you signals of pain and stiffness. If you continue to push for the impossible, you may eventually find yourself wrapped in bandages instead of your dance clothes.

Going underdressed in a cold studio is dangerous from another point of view: As you work (slowly and carefully when it's cold), you will finally get warmed up and you may even begin to sweat. Without enough covering, the cold air will have free rein to rush to the moisture on the surface of your skin and lower your body temperature rapidly. As soon as you stop moving, you'll cool down dramatically. This will put a strain on your body systems and make you susceptible to muscle spasms and chills. On a cold day it's not a bad idea to take a pair of warm-up tights and a sweater along in your dance bag, just in case the studio turns out not to be well heated. Then you have an alternative.

Many dancers wear warm-up garments in hot weather as well as cold, and I've seen students in class wearing full woolen body suits when the temperature outside was ninety degrees. I even tried it a few times myself, with the result that I felt faint at the end of class because I had lost so much body fluid through perspiration. Each of us has different needs and different tolerances for heat. You'll have to read your own thermostat and decide what's best for you. But do be careful about becoming overly dependent on warm-up clothes or using them when you don't really need to.

Hair

When you think of a ballerina, you probably envision a woman standing on her toes with a neat bun at the back of her head. And when you imagine a premier danseur, you're likely to think of someone like Nureyev or Baryshnikov, who have relatively short hair. There's no need for you to have a bun if you're a woman or to keep your hair short if you're a man, but, whether you're male or female, if you have long hair you'll want to give some thought to what you do with it in class.

Stunning as your lengthy tresses may be, you'll be better off in dance class tying them back or pinning them to your head. Ballet, modern, jazz, and tap all make use of the head, more vigorously in some cases than in others. In ballet you simply can't do certain steps (rapid, successive turns, for instance) without having your hair firmly in place, and under any circumstances you can go seriously askew if your eyes are suddenly draped with a blinding curtain of hair. For theatrical effect while performing, you may want your hair down; but, generally speaking, for classes you'll be safer, more comfortable, and better off overall if you keep your hair arranged neatly.

Especially copious hair may be a challenge to keep together and back, and you may find it necessary to use strength and patience to achieve your goals of a smooth, secure assemblage. For my long hair I first bind a ponytail at the back of my head with a shoelace (rubber bands break). Then I use three super-size barrettes to bolt down the overflow. The benefits to my dancing far outweigh the investment of materials, time, and effort.

Any barrettes you use to pin your hair should have a strong catch so that they won't become lethal projectiles should they come loose (while doing fast turns, for example). Large hairpins and decorative combs are susceptible to flying out of your hair, too. Even if they don't hit anyone, they can land on the floor in a place where another student or you yourself may later step and slip on them.

How you wear your hair may also disguise problems in the carriage of your head or the alignment of your back. If you allow your hair to billow out around your face, neck, and shoulders, you'll lose an opportunity for the teacher to correct your alignment as needed. Wearing kerchiefs and scarves can also camouflage the head-to-neck relationship, but if you find that's the only way to control your hair, a small, neat arrangement that follows the contour of your head is best.

When I first started dancing, a female dancer with short hair was something of an oddity. I even heard about one choreographer who threatened to cast out from the company any woman who had the audacity to crop her crowning glory. Thank goodness for the liberation we've had since that time. Short hair is as acceptable as long for female dancers, and much more manageable for the curly-headed among us. For safety's sake, the only precaution you need follow with short hair is to keep the top pieces pinned back so that they won't swipe your eyes at inopportune moments.

Jewelry

Aunt Sadie's heirloom bracelet and matching brooch may look gorgeous on you, and the one-pound gold neck chain the woman in your life gave you for Christmas may be something you just don't want to take off, but they probably won't help your dancing much and can present a hazard in class. Any jewelry is a potential weapon—against either you or your fellow students. Earrings can fly off, bracelets and wristwatches can gouge crevices, necklaces can strangle, pins can pierce and stick, and you can use your imagination about the impact of boulder-size jewels or rings when they make contact with another student or a part of your own body. If you simply can't get through class without a bauble or two on your person, choose small, discreet ones that won't be a menace to anyone.

Some teachers will tell you that heavy bracelets also affect your work in class by putting extra weight at the ends of your arms. The carriage of your arms is an important ingredient in your technique, and you probably should remove bracelets before class for this reason.

*F*eet

You undoubtedly learned, as I did, that in dressing your feet, your socks go on first, then your shoes. Would it make any sense to you to put socks, shoes, and then more socks on? Some ballet dancers seem to think so.* Anything you wear on your feet goes, so long as it's appropriate for the type of class you're taking and doesn't turn the floor into ice or flypaper. Your dancing will suffer either way, whether your contact with the floor is too slick or too sticky.

MODERN CLASSES

The safest and most common foot condition for modern classes is *au naturel*—in bare feet. You can buy modern dance tights that end at your ankles, thereby leaving your feet bare; if you have the kind with feet attached, you'll want to cut them off (or cut only the toes and heels out of the feet if you like the stirrup effect). Although most modern dancers go barefoot, there is a special sandal you can wear. It's useful on some types of studio floors, or if you've injured your foot. When buying a pair, your only criterion for fit should be absolute comfort. The sandals should not bind your feet at any place, nor should they swim on you. Generally, you can expect you won't need any shoes in a modern class, however.

BALLET CLASSES

Soft ballet shoes. For ballet class, you should have ballet slippers, although some dancers do take the first part of the class at the barre in bare feet or just socks, because they feel their feet work better that way. Once you start moving across the floor, though, you're in dangerous territory. If you're barefoot you

* Often ballet dancers wear socks over new shoes to break them in during class and at the same time keep them clean for performance. But the practice has been arbitrarily adopted by many students who are neither breaking in new shoes nor about to perform in them.

open yourself up to injuring the bottoms of your feet from the rosin on most ballet-studio floors, and if you're in socks you may experience an unanticipated landing. Falling needn't be the worst experience of your dancing career, but it's known to break bones and cause other types of discomfort you'll probably want to avoid.

Soft ballet shoes are made by several manufacturers in various lasts and degrees of sturdiness ranging from boardlike to extremely supple, depending on the type of sole. Both leather and canvas styles are available. The last and fabric of the shoe you wear are extremely important to how your feet work and therefore to your technique, so you should be careful about selecting them. You should probably experiment with different kinds until you find the type you dance best in; also keep in mind that as your feet strengthen you may want to change the type of shoe you wear.

Most dancers I know prefer the leather rather than the canvas ballet shoe, because leather gives your feet greater support. To wear the canvas type your foot must be very strong and well put together; otherwise, you'll find your feet strain as you work in them. A "Russian" ballet shoe, with a thicker, less pliable sole, is also hard for some dancers to work in. Although it's made for either men or women, men wear it more often, because it provides greater support when you land from jumps. In a Russian shoe you have to work your feet especially hard to make them point well, and this may not be the best condition for development of your particular body.

The length of the vamp of your ballet shoes also affects how you work in them. Many students find they dance best in a high vamp that hugs the top part of the foot. Other dancers prefer a lower vamp.

In addition to the fact that ballet shoes differ according to manufacturer, last, and materials used, you must also consider that there's a human element involved in their making. Each pair is shaped and sewn at some point in the manufacturing process by the hands of an operator (whom I like to imagine as petite, loving, and devoted). That's why, even when you buy the same kind of shoes from the same manufacturer again and again, you'll find one pair will be different from another, depending on which operator worked on them.

New ballet shoes should be very snug but not crippling. Leather ones stretch out enormously after you've worn them a few times, and will feel like galoshes if you haven't bought them small enough. But don't buy them so small that they'll bruise and blister your feet or split apart on the first jump you take in them. Canvas shoes shouldn't be as snug as leather, because they don't stretch out as much.

A good guide for fit is to put the shoes on and rise to the balls of your feet. If you have significant difficulty and discomfort doing this, the shoes are too small. Another test is to point your foot strongly while it's off the floor in front of you. If you see a very large gap along the arch of your foot, the shoes are too big. If you're having trouble deciding between one size and the next, take the larger. If they turn out to be a bit too large after they're broken in, you can always wear a pair of thick socks inside to fill up the space. Shoes that are too small create many more problems and you may have to throw them out in the end.

If you have a pair of feet that just won't fit into any regular stock shoes, you may want to have some custom-made. Not all ballet-shoe manufacturers offer this service, so you'll have to ask about it at a dance-supply store.

When you're buying your first pair of ballet shoes, shop around before you settle on any. Try different manufacturers and different sizes and ask the salesperson's advice (though sometimes, depending on his or her experience, you can't count on it). Usually a store will give you return privileges if you tell them you'd like your teacher to check out the fit before you use the shoes. Then you can take them to class for your teacher's professional advice.

To break in a pair of ballet shoes so that you don't torture your feet or lose your investment due to their ripping open, I suggest the following regime:

If they are the first pair you've ever owned, wear them around the house for fifteen to thirty minutes on two or three different days before you use them in class. Put a pair of light cotton or nylon socks on your feet before you put the shoes on, to prevent any rubbing or blisters on your skin, and then walk around.

If you're replacing an old pair of ballet shoes with new ones, you can break them in at home or take them with you to class to do it. You should: (1) start to break in your new shoes before your old ones are in tatters; (2) wear the new ones when you go to the barre in class, but carry your old pair with you; (3) wear the new shoes until your feet begin to tire; then (4) put your old shoes on for the rest of the class. You'll probably get through fifteen or twenty minutes in the new pair, but in the next class you'll get further.

You can also prevent your shoes from coming apart at the seams and make each pair last longer by switching them from left to right, probably alternating with each class. This may seem strange at first, accustomed as you are to wearing a left shoe on your left foot and a right one on your right. Ballet slippers are designed to be a kind of second skin on your foot, though, and aren't made in a left or right shape. They'll change their conformation from one to the other quite readily. This system works for many dancers, but you may not be able to put it into operation until your feet are quite strong. And it's also possible that the shape and structure of your feet won't adapt to it easily. You can try it, though, and see what happens.

Pointe shoes. Pointe shoes are an even more personal matter than soft ballet shoes. Ballerinas dream about the perfect pair, and sometimes—maybe once in a lifetime—they do come along. But—poof!—after one performance they're useless. Depending on how much you dance on pointe and how strong your feet are, you'll be able to wear your pointe shoes for quite a few classes. If your pointe work is only occasional, or if you're just beginning pointe, a pair can last for months. Of course, you won't last in them unless they fit properly and have the right degree of sturdiness or suppleness for your feet.

Pointe shoes vary with the manufacturer, the last, and the individual operator who's involved in making them. If you're buying your first pair, you'll need all the professional help you can get from your teacher and other dancers you know. To this day I remain grateful to Diana Cartier of the Joffrey Ballet, who suggested Freeds for my feet, But one dancer's meat is another's poison. In the end you're the one who's going to suffer or survive in your pointe shoes, so don't rush or be pressured into buying any that overly excite your pain threshhold. Here, again, ask the store about return privileges and have your teacher check the fit.

Men sometimes work in pointe shoes because it builds strength in the feet and back and also helps straighten and strengthen the legs. Women's-size shoes may fit, but if your foot's a bit larger you can have them custom-made.

Everyone seems to have a personal technique for breaking in pointe shoes. I've heard some dancers say they put the toe box of the shoe into the space between the hinged side of a door and the molding, then slam the door shut. Another method to soften the toe box is to beat it with a hammer. Other dancers say they just bend the shank of the shoe back a little and then wear them around the house a few times before class. Find out what your teacher recommends.

Elastics and ribbons. Both soft ballet shoes and pointe shoes need to have elastics and/or ribbons sewn on before you wear them in class. Techniques and preferences for doing this vary so widely that it's hard to say which you'll like best. Ask your teacher about it.

JAZZ CLASSES

Jazz shoes are deliciously soft leather lace-ups with an almost-flat heel that places your weight a bit forward, gives you a deeper plié, and helps get you moving a bit more easily. The shoe is designed to give support while allowing your feet maximum freedom of movement, and it should fit you closely but comfortably. Jazz shoes shouldn't require any serious break-in regime.

You don't absolutely have to wear jazz shoes for most jazz classes. Many students use their ballet shoes, sneakers, or bare feet, and I've even seen stiletto-heeled knee-high boots on dancers who have their own special approach to class. If you're just beginning, and to be kind to your ankles, calf muscles, and lower back, I suggest a less precarious flat-heeled arrangement.

TAP CLASSES

For tap class you'll definitely want taps. You don't necessarily need to buy the special shoes normally used for tap; any pair you already own will do so long as they fit well, have rather short, thick, or flat heels, will stay securely on your feet, and look as though they'll withstand regular beating. If you have such a pair, you can buy just taps and have your shoemaker affix them to the soles and heels, using screws rather than nails and placing the front tap on the sole so that it projects about an eighth of an inch beyond the front of the shoe. You may also want a piece of treaded, no-slip rubber attached to the part of the sole that the tap doesn't cover.

Dance-supply stores sell different types of taps: the basic, plain flat metal type and the staccato type that you may be mad for; it has a second metal flap on it to give an extra jingling sound. If you elect to buy the special shoes dance-supply stores sell, you'll find them in kid or patent leather and either flat or with a higher heel. Try on enough pairs to be sure beyond a doubt that they're not biting your heels or crunching your toes. You'll be putting a lot of poundage down on your feet in tap, and you'll want to be reasonably comfortable doing so.

Where to Buy Dance Clothes and Shoes

Most large department stores stock leotards and tights that are either expressly made for dancing or will serve just as well. Hosiery stores are another good source. To find stores where dance clothes and shoes are a specialty, look in the Yellow Pages for your city under the heading "Dancing Supplies." Many cities now have a Capezio or a Selva store. You can look these up in the white pages. And you can also check *Dance Magazine* for ads placed by dance-supply stores and mail-order houses.

Some stores give a discount to students and professionals, so be sure to ask about it. Also be on the lookout for bargain stores or manufacturers' outlets that sell dance clothes at reduced prices.[7]

5

The Dancer's Bill of Fare:
Nutrition and Rest

Nutrition

You've probably reached the time in your life when you're finally free of having someone tell you to eat your spinach and clean your plate. I'm not going to try to drag you back to those days, but I am going to give you the facts about nutrition: what it means to your dancing and how to manage your diet so that you meet your basic nutritional needs as a dancer.

Of course, straight facts aren't always enough. Food can be a strange part of our lives, laden with all sorts of psychological and emotional associations. The issue is complicated also because scientists simply don't know everything about how the body in general or any one body in particular actually uses food. I've tried to present here as much as is currently known (or surmised) about nutrition for dancers, and I've attempted to keep it as free as possible from pet theories I've heard from dancers and other sources that may or may not have some basis in physiological fact.

Aside from the content of this chapter, though, and beyond any food trip you may be into, there's an important overview that you should keep in mind: Good nutrition serves both your short-term and long-term needs as a dancer. On a daily basis it keeps you going in classes, rehearsals, and at any job you might have. It keeps both your mind and your muscles alert for action. For long-term development it builds your muscles, makes your body systems operate better, and helps prevent or hasten your recovery from injuries. In other words, what you eat is of monumental importance to how you dance.

THE BASICS

Everyone, dancers included, needs the six basics: carbohydrate, fat, protein, minerals, vitamins, and water. You can get them by eating well-balanced meals, or even a series of snacks through the day that add up to a well-balanced overall diet. In practical terms a well-balanced diet means taking in calories that approximate these ratios: 50–55 percent carbohydrate; 35–40 percent fat; 10–15 percent protein. These percentages and the actual quantities of food you need vary with your sex, age, height, weight, bone structure, and metabolic rate. There is no one formula that fits everyone precisely. A nutritionist can come close to saying what a balanced diet means for you, but even that won't be perfect. Meanwhile, if you want a rough estimate of what your needs are, use a nutrition or calorie-counting book that has charts describing the nutritional content of foods and the prescribed intake for your sex, age, height, and weight.[8]

If calorie- and gram-counting bores you as much as it does me, you can approach nutrition via the shotgun approach: Eat as wide a variety of food as you can so that meat, poultry, fish, vegetables, fruit, milk, and grains (like bread and cereal) all have a chance on a fair and distributed basis to give you their nutrients.

The only items you should very actively avoid are foods with large amounts of artificial additives; junk foods such as soda, candy, potato chips, corn cheesies, and taco chips; and other empty-calorie foods like alcohol. These take up room in your diet that would be better used by nutritious foods. In some cases they even devour vitamins your body needs for normal functioning. Excessive alcohol depletes Vitamin B, and potato chips can do away with Vitamin E when they're rancid, which they often are. Another disadvantage of junk foods is that many are made with palm and coconut oils, which are highly saturated fats and therefore undesirable in your diet.

Vitamins and minerals are present in almost all foods that aren't junk foods, so you don't have to make a special point of calculating them so long as you follow a varied diet. As for water, remember to drink it especially if you've perspired heavily during class. It may seem unnecessary to make this reminder, because normally you'll be thirsty after a very sweaty class. However, in some cases your degree of thirst won't be a clear indicator of the amount of water your body needs and you'll have to make an active choice about drinking it. (Be careful, though, not to gulp large quantities immediately after class; it can give you stomach cramps. Take small sips spaced over a few minutes.)

There are so many theories and books about nutrition that I won't go any further in giving general recommendations, except for one. If you're considering changing your basic eating habits, be sure that you are well informed and that you give your body enough time to adjust. This applies, for instance, if you've eaten meat most of your life and are now thinking about vegetarianism. Don't make any such change drastically or without a good book or a nutritionist's directives.

SPECIAL NEEDS OF DANCERS

Meals versus snacks. The standard three-meals-a-day routine may not work for you, especially if your schedule is hectic. You can't eat any large meals just before class; in fact, you have to allow about three hours between a really big meal and a class. At the same time, you need to keep up your energy. As I've already mentioned, individual needs vary, and you should probably experiment to find what works for you. Here's some information that you can put to use while you're testing out various alternatives.

Breakfast. It's supposed to be a good idea to have breakfast—not a large one necessarily, but something that is more than just coffee and orange juice and that gives you enough carbohydrate to burn for the first activities of the day. It shouldn't consist exclusively of carbohydrate, either, but should include some protein and fat as well.

Lunch and dinner. It doesn't matter if you have a formal lunch or dinner so long as you take in what your body needs at the right times. If you do have lunch prior to a class, make it a fairly light one an hour to an hour and a half beforehand, and try not to go rushing madly about after you eat. Most dancers wait to have dinner until classes or rehearsals are over for the day. This is fine provided you have either lunch or a snack about an hour before your class or rehearsal.

Before a performance. Eating before performance is a very tricky and personal affair. Some dancers won't touch a meal throughout the entire day, having only snacks until after the performance is over. Others eat a huge steak about three hours before curtain time.

Carbohydrate snacks. Carbohydrate—sugar and starch—is sometimes referred to as "brain food." (Fish is, too, but in the long-term sense. Carbohydrate is for more immediate use.) For dancers carbohydrate serves as both brain and muscle food; if you dance, you just can't function without it. A light carbohydrate snack that you can digest quickly is good about an hour before classes or rehearsals and when you're in the midst of a long rehearsal and feel you're fading fast. It should contain an adequate but not excessive amount of carbohydrate. Bombarding your system with a high dose of it can cause your insulin-producing mechanism to overreact, resulting in a "low" after your first energy "high." You will need to find out for yourself what adequate-but-not-excessive means to your body. Be aware, however, that you can create an unstable condition if you put too much carbohydrate into your system at one time.

Snacks that many dancers find provide them with the right amount of carbohydrate are yogurt, milk, fresh fruit, fresh vegetables, and juice. All of these are speedily digested, rapidly leave your stomach, and quickly reach your head and muscles in amounts your body can handle comfortably.

Candy and cookies are also sources of carbohydrate, but the excessive sugar content often zaps your system unnecessarily and stands without the redeeming features of nutritive ingredients like protein, vitamins, and minerals. What you may wind up with instead are difficult-to-digest fats, unnecessary additives and preservatives, and extra calories. Especially when you're trying to keep your weight down while providing your body with the necessary carbohydrate, you're best off ignoring candy, cookies, and cake.

Incidentally, whether you eat it as a snack or as part of a meal, yogurt is a good all-around food for dancers. It has a substantial carbohydrate content, is low in calories, and is also a good source of fat, protein, and the calcium that your muscles must have for contraction. (Most manufacturers print calorie and nutritional information right on the container, in case you want to check on the amounts.)

Protein. You may have heard somewhere along the line that

dancers should have extra protein in their diet. Recent research says that's not necessarily the case.[9] If your food intake is well balanced, you're probably already eating enough protein. Though it's not conclusive, there has been additional evidence recently that excess amounts deplete your body's supply of calcium. If you follow the basic 10-to-15-percent rule of thumb for protein intake, you won't run this risk. You also won't have the problem of protein usurping the space in your diet that should be used for carbohydrate and fat.

Vitamin and mineral supplements. Here again, much research remains to be done. The few things that do seem to be clear are that extra doses of vitamins change the way your body operates. E, for example, slows the aging process (which actually isn't a bad idea for dancers), and C is supposed to be good for stress, both physical and mental (though the common-cold controversy continues and some researchers say that massive doses are harmful). A and D have both been shown to be toxic in large amounts, so be careful in taking them.

Salt-tablet supplements relieve muscle cramps when you've been sweating a great deal. Other than that, there's nothing absolutely conclusive to report about the beneficial effects of extra minerals in your diet.

Keep in mind that taking large quantities of anything holds the potential of upsetting your body's delicate chemical balance. Check with a nutrition expert before you go full steam ahead with any high-dose programs.

Weight control. I guess it has something to do with looking in the mirror so much when you're a dancer and being generally very conscious of your physical self that turns excess weight into the bane of your existence. Extra weight doesn't help you move around easily, either, but a pound or two usually doesn't make all that much difference. Nonetheless, if you dance it's more than likely that at some point or other you'll start thinking about how to lose weight.

A good guideline to follow is that decreasing your food intake by 500 calories a day will enable you to lose half a pound every three days. Also be guided by the general rule that it's not healthy to lose more than two or three pounds a week. If you do, the weight is less likely to stay off, and such a rapid loss can be damaging.

Crash diets are definitely out for the active dancer. They make you listless and weak and limit your ability to concentrate. Fad diets such as the high-protein regime that became popular several years ago give the same result. A dancer simply needs ready energy in the form of carbohydrate and cannot get by with protein alone.

If you're looking for carbohydrate with a reasonable number of calories, you can again turn to a nutrition book as a source. Until you find one that you like, here are some figures you can use: [10]

	FOOD	CALORIES	GRAMS OF CARBOHYDRATE
Group 1	Banana (2 large, about 7 ounces each)	232	60
	Brownie (4.5 ounces)	484	68
	Chocolate candy (4 ounces)	588	64
Group 2	Apple	80	20
	Bagel	165	30
Group 3	Orange juice (8.8 ounces)	110	26
	Chocolate cake with icing (4.2 ounces)	443	67

Look closely at the foods in Group 1 on the chart, and you'll notice that you are hit with more than twice as many calories and derive only 8 more grams of carbohydrate when you eat one 4.5-ounce brownie as compared to two 7-ounce bananas. If you put a 4-ounce piece of chocolate candy in your mouth, the calorie count goes up by 100 and your carbohydrate consumption drops by 4 grams. For half the calories of the bagel in Group 2, you get two-thirds the carbohydrate by eating an apple instead. And in Group 3, a glass of orange juice totals only one-quarter the number of calories but gives you nearly half the carbohydrate in a piece of chocolate cake.

Of course, when you decrease your caloric intake you'll want to continue with a balanced diet and not spend all your allotted calories on carbohydrate. You can also increase the amount of exercise you do—dance and other. This will help you lose weight. Remember, too, that a bulge here or there might respond to spot-reducing exercises, so you can try those.

Rest

Caught up in the flurry of your dance classes, job, social life, and other activities, you may occasionally forget to honor your body's need for rest. The problem is that unless you ease up from time to time, your muscles will tighten and you'll increase the probability of injury. James Waring used to say (with a knowing grin) that the only proper activities for a dancer were dancing and lying down. But it's difficult to get through life doing only those two things.

Sleep is one perfect form of rest, but individual dancers' needs for it vary widely. I know some dancers who hit the sack for nine or ten hours every night, or at least three times a week. Others function energetically on six or seven a night. Performing will change your sleep needs, too.

The best barometer by which to gauge your need for sleep is your energy level. If you find yourself dragging at the same hour each day (and you're eating a balanced diet and enough carbohydrate), more sleep at night or perhaps a nap might be in order.

Not with my schedule, you say? Try taking your schedule apart to see if there isn't something that can be eliminated or at least pared down. It's really worth it, because your body and your mind will work best for dancing when you give them the rest (and nourishment) they so richly merit for serving you well.

Rest can mean more than sleep, too. It can mean getting away for a few days, maybe even a week, or taking a break from classes. A dancer I know used to take class seven days a week: two every day except on Sundays, when she took only one. She was terrified of losing her technique. An injury forced her off her feet for a week, and when she returned to class she was amazed to find her already-high leg extensions soaring beyond their previous levels and her muscles working with new and welcome fluidity.

You can also snatch some moments of intensive rest by doing yoga or meditation exercises that are specially designed for deep mental and physical relaxation. You can find out more about these through books or classes. You may also want to try something called "constructive rest," in which it's possible to feel totally refreshed after just five or ten minutes of lying on your back with your arms crossed, knees bent, and soles of your feet on the floor while you think of certain "constructive" body images.[11]

Whether it's sleep, a change of routine, or deep relaxation, giving your body and mind a rest is the best way to keep your entire being in balance. You simply can't work all the time and expect a sustained high level of physical and mental performance. Just as you need music and meter for dance class, so do your body and mind need to achieve a harmonious rhythm of work and relaxation.[12] Balance is different for each individual, of course, but most dancers are such dedicated, motivated, hardworking, energetic people that they sometimes forget or feel guilty about getting rest. Consider these paragraphs a reminder and a license for yourself.

6

In Action:
Putting Your Body
to Work

Dancing puts your body to use in ways that other forms of exercise do not. It requires strength and flexibility as well as grace and coordination, stamina and fortitude as well as fluidity and softness. In learning to dance, you'll ask your body to do what it's never done before, and you'll strive to use it with a fullness you never thought possible. All of this can cause destructive stresses and strains unless you work correctly. There are basic concepts about the human body that apply no matter what type or style of dance you study. If you understand and use these concepts, you can both dance better and avoid harming your body.

From time to time you'll hear heroic stories about professional dancers who carry on with injuries, bandaged and anesthetized, going on to perform when thinking mortals would lie in bed. Edward Villella of the New York City Ballet is reputed to have continued performing with hairline fractures in the metatarsal bones of his foot, and I'm sure he's not the only one who's done it. This may inspire awe, but once we're through being impressed we should remember that it's not important to be a hero or heroine to dance. You should look to dancing to give you a strong, healthy, attractive body that functions marvelously and provides a constant source of delight. Sure, you'll have some aches and pains, and if you dance a great deal you'll wonder why you put up with the physical demands at all. But in the end you'll find that you love dancing more than you hate the minor discomforts.

Working Correctly

I would guess that there are a few dancers who believe, as I once did, that injuries are caused primarily by accidents: slipping, tripping, running into someone or something, forgetting to point your foot at the right instant and inadvertently twisting your ankle. But the longer I've danced, the more I've understood that accidents are quite rare as causes of dance injuries. The majority of injuries are caused—and prevented—by how you work at your dancing, consistently and over time. Working incorrectly just once usually won't hurt you; your body is quite resilient and can bounce back from some amount of abuse. But if you work incorrectly again and again, class after class, performance after performance, day after day, and year after year, your body—or some part of it—will finally give out. It will simply refuse to function anymore. You don't ever have to reach that point, no matter how long you dance, and this material on working correctly aims to help you avoid it.

WORKING WITHIN THE CONTEXT OF YOUR OWN BODY STRUCTURE

Dance depends on the basics of anatomy and physiology that we all have in common. Certain mechanical principles of movement apply in all dance techniques, based on the way bodies are normally put together and function. For instance, you have much more freedom of movement in your shoulder than you do in your hip because of the way these joints are formed. Principles of movement and technique apply to you just as they do to any other normal human being. Because your body isn't exactly like any other, however, these principles will apply to you in a slightly different way. By learning to know your body—listening to its messages and perceiving its various sensations—you stand the best chance of working within its structure and thereby avoiding stresses, strains, and injuries.

Everyone's basic equipment is recognizably the same, but there are enough variations, both anatomically and physiologically, to make one person's body messages like those of no other body. Take muscles, for instance. Almost everyone has the same ones lying in approximately the same positions and attaching to the same bones. There are some muscles, though (and bones and connective tissue as well), that are present in most people but absent in others. There is wide variation also in the length of muscles and in overall mass and strength.

Physiologically, there is again a basic universality in such functions as digestion, circulation, nerve impulse, and glandular activity. The stomach processes food to make it available for use by the body's cells; the heart pumps blood, sending nutrients and oxygen to the cells and carrying away wastes; nervous impulses cause muscles and other body mechanisms to work; and glands help to regulate body processes overall. But there are differences from one person to another in all these: Digestion can be faster or slower, more efficient or less; circulation can be sluggish or good; the nerves can be hair-triggered or serene; and endocrine glands can secrete just enough, too much, or too little hormone. In the end, all these differences add up to a physical, mental, and emotional being who is like no other.

Following are some examples to get you started thinking about how your body might vary and how to become attuned to its messages.

Every dancer at some time or another will sit on the floor with the soles of the feet together and the knees dropped out to the sides. If you go into a class and compare students doing this, you'll see knees at every imaginable angle. Some students will have them up around waist height, and at the other extreme will be those with thighs resting along the floor. In some modern techniques you do exercises in this position, such as forward bounces with the torso, designed to loosen the thigh sockets and stretch out the lower back. When doing this exercise, your attention should be on these two areas of your body. If you sense a loosening in the sockets and a stretch in the back, then you're on the right track. But if your sockets are a bit tighter and your knees set at a relatively high angle, you may have to make some adjustments before you begin feeling the right sensations. You may have to move your feet forward, to lift a bit more along the sides of the rib cage, to remember to keep breathing easily as you do the bounces. Your objective shouldn't be to get your knees closer to the floor, like the person to your left. You can strain your hip joints trying to do that. Rather, you should focus on the sensations of loosening and stretching. You might look different from the outside, but so long as the right sensations are there, you're achieving the intended results of the exercise.

Leg extensions are another example. Go to any dance class and you'll see legs lifted to every conceivable height, from knee level to earlobe-high and beyond. In leg extensions the object is to lift your leg and place it at the right line in relation to your hip socket, but not at the expense of the length of your torso or the position of your hips. As soon as you collapse your torso or let your hips fly around, you limit your body's overall freedom of movement. If your leg isn't placed properly in relation to your hip, you'll also cause your muscles to strain in keeping it up.

When you do an exercise that involves lifting your leg, you'll want to feel sensations of length, breath, hip position, and a lack of straining in the muscles. The fact that your teacher's or a fellow student's leg is lifted above hip height doesn't mean that yours has to be. The important things for you to concentrate on involve the principles of efficient movement: The muscles raising your leg should feel as though they're working but not straining, your torso should feel long and full of breath, and your hips should feel as though they're participating in the movement together (not as though the hip of the extended leg has become detached from the hip of the other leg). Your leg may seem discouragingly low when you begin to work correctly, but your overall appearance will be far more pleasing and your physical performance more effective than if you violate the structure of your body.

Yet another difference you'll encounter among dancers is the degree to which their legs will turn out in the hip sockets. Some students make the mistake of trying to turn out from the feet rather than from the hips. They see another student's or the teacher's feet at a certain angle and infer that theirs must be the same. Ballet is based on the principle that turnout from the hips permits technical performance that is otherwise impossible. It's not necessary to turn your feet out to the same position on the floor as anyone else's, only to turn out fully in *your* hips, keeping your knees and ankles properly lined up below. When you turn out your legs you must *sense* that the turnout is happening in your hips and not in your feet or knees.

You derive no mechanical advantage unless turnout comes from the hips, and in fact you weaken the ankle and knee joints and create the potential for such injuries as sprains and torn knee cartilages. Even though your turnout may at first look disappointing to you, it will work as efficiently as anyone else's provided you think about achieving it at the hips and keep your knees and feet properly in line. Turnout increases and becomes more secure as you continue working correctly within the context of your own body.

ALIGNMENT

Poor alignment is a major cause of stress and strain on the muscles and joints of the body. Alignment refers to how the bones of your skeleton stack up: your skull on top of your spine, the individual vertebrae of your spine on top of each other, your rib cage above your pelvis, your knees under your hips, and your ankles and feet under your knees.

The bones of your skeleton are held in place by ligaments and muscles. When the ligaments are in good elastic condition and the muscles are well toned but not tense, the chances of having good skeletal alignment are excellent. Muscles are the principal determining factor in alignment, however, and they are subject to various influences. If you're nervous, for instance, your muscles will be tense. Some of them will be more tense than others, and these will pull the bones they are attached to out of line. With some people it's the muscles in the back of the neck that tense up when they're nervous and that pull the skull back off its nice, easy resting place at the top of the spine.

Nervous tension isn't the only factor that affects alignment, however. Mood does too. If you're depressed or down in the dumps, and you walk around with downcast eyes to reflect your low spirits, it will pull your head forward.

There are social influences on people's "carriage," as well. It used to be fashionable, for instance, to stand in a "model's slump," with the back and shoulders rounded forward, the chest sunken, and the pelvis tipped under. I can't begin to describe the havoc this plays with joints and muscles (not to mention internal organs). There's massive confusion about which muscles should be used to hold what, which joint should bear what weight, and what poor ligaments should be stretched to their limits.

The wrong ideas about "good posture" also may affect alignment. The idea of "standing straight," for example, runs directly contrary to the anatomical fact that your spine has several natural curves in it that are essential to good alignment. Pulling your shoulders back, as in a military stance, is also against the body's natural grain, which is to have shoulders and arms hang nicely and easily from the top of the rib cage, rather than to be held backward and up off it.

Habits, moods, personality, and ideas can all result in skeletal alignment that doesn't put your body at its best for dancing (or many other life activities, for that matter). Poor alignment puts stresses and strains on joints and muscles under any circumstance, but when you add dancing to your list of activities you compound the problems that improper alignment would cause in any case.

With poor alignment muscles are forced to work beyond their reasonable capacity, joints become bogged down with more weight than they were designed to bear, and the ligaments that bind joints together are stretched so far that they lose their natural elasticity. None of this has to happen if you work on your alignment conscientiously and remember that finding and maintaining it are a never-ending process, affected by day-to-day fluctuations in everything from the bills that arrive in the mail to the weather. Just as your body is living, growing, and ever-changing, so must you expect your alignment to be. But don't let this be discouraging, for there are a number of ways to work productively at it.

Achieving good alignment. Your regular teacher should be a good source of help with your alignment. He or she will watch you in class and offer suggestions on how to place your head or your pelvis and how the body parts should relate to each other when you're standing still and when you're moving. Ballet and modern dance teachers are in many cases more concerned with teaching alignment than jazz or tap teachers, primarily because the body line is considered more important in ballet and modern dance. Alignment is as critical to jazz and tap techniques, though, when it comes down to protecting your body against stresses and strains. Thus, if you're principally a jazz or tap dance student and alignment doesn't seem to be one of your regular teacher's class topics, you might want to try a ballet or modern class where it's addressed.

In addition to ballet and modern dance teachers who incorporate alignment instruction into their regular classes, there are teachers who specialize in "corrective" or "therapeutic" alignment classes. These teachers may or may not teach dance and will use floor exercises and other techniques (including relaxation) to put your skeleton back on the right track. If you feel you're really in need of some serious alignment work, your best bet in finding one of these teachers is to ask your regular teacher or other dancers at the studio where you normally take classes. You might also try some of the suggestions in Chapter 1 of this book.

Chiropractors are a never-ending source of conversation for dancers, and many of my dancer friends say they wouldn't be dancing today if they hadn't received chiropractic "adjustments." A chiropractor works on the alignment of the vertebrae in your spine, helping them through physical manipulation to keep their proper places underneath each other. Since there are many muscles that connect to your spine, and many nerves that enter and exit from the central nervous system between the vertebrae, the effects of these adjustments can sometimes be quite dramatic and full of long-sought relief.

There's a standing dispute between M.D.'s and chiropractors, however, and if you've been exposed to this controversy you may be skeptical. I believe that each person has to judge individually for him or herself whether a chiropractor is warranted. Consider it an alternative that you may want to investigate if you haven't already done so.

You can also work on your alignment through the use of "mental images." Lulu Sweigard's *Human Movement Potential*[13] and Mable Elsworth Todd's book, *The Thinking Body*,[14] both explain and explore this technique for improving alignment. Chapter 11 in this book also deals with the topic.

Spinal, head, and pelvic alignment are particular focal points for dancers, but equally important is the lineup of your knees and feet. To maintain their proper alignment, you'll want to be careful not to "roll in" on the inside arches of your feet. This applies whether you're standing with your knees straight or bent or with your legs turned in or out. One way to tell if you're rolling in on your arches is to notice whether the outer edges of your feet (the little-toe sides) feel as though they're carrying less weight than the inner edges (the big-toe sides). Another clue is to check on whether your little toes seem to be coming off the floor; if so, you're bound to be rolling in.

When your knees are bent, as in a plié, a good check is to look down and note whether your knees are pointing outward directly over the toes. If they seem to angle inward toward the big-toe side of the foot, your arches are rolled in.

Ask your teacher for help with the problem of rolling arches. He or she may give you special strengthening exercises to do, or may work out other ways to enable you to correct the alignment of your lower legs and feet.

Many dance students develop what is called a "ballet dancer's walk" after they've danced for a few years. Less euphemistically, it's referred to as a "duck walk." The feet move forward pointing sideways instead of straight. Although it requires determination, even a dancer who has taken ballet class for years can train him or herself to walk with the feet pointing dead ahead. Walking with your feet straight actually helps to strengthen the muscles that act on the knee and foot—for both turned-out and turned-in positions—and also prevents deteriorative stretching of the ligaments that bind these joints together. From personal experience I know it's difficult if you take ballet class consistently. But it's supposed to be a good way to protect your knees and ankles from unnecessary stresses and strains.

PLACEMENT

Alignment is really a part of placement. Once your bones are lined up it's time to start thinking about the other ingredient of placement, which is where your total body weight is.

You can rock your weight forward over your toes or backward over your heels. Slight as the difference may seem, placing your weight a bit forward or backward seriously affects how all your muscles and joints operate. When your weight is too far back, even though you can dance with it there, the placement sets up a stressful condition. When your weight is too far forward, you'll tend to "break" in the hip line, pushing your hips behind your chest and putting pressure on your knee joints and lower back.

You can work for placement in several of the same ways you can for alignment: through your regular teacher, specialized teachers, ballet and modern teachers, and through the use of techniques such as are suggested by Sweigard and Todd.

In ordinary walking, too, you should be conscious of where your total body weight falls with each step. The more consistent your placement is in all your activities, the better it will carry over to your dancing, enabling you to prevent stress and strain.

YOUR CENTER

Much dancing may look like it's all arms and legs. To dance really well, though, and without unduly taxing your body, you must learn to move everything—including arms and legs, which look so peripheral—from your center.

The concept of "center" refers to the center of gravity in your body—an imaginary point somewhere within the interior of your pelvis. Everyone's center is in a slightly different place because of variations in weight and body structure. As Irene Dowd defines it, your center is ". . . the point around which the entire body weight balances equally above and below, and to all sides."[15] She likens the center of gravity in your body to the hub of a wheel, with all the moving parts around it being spokes.

A dancer who has a strong sense of center seems to control his or her limbs through muscle action that begins in the pelvis. A leg may look spectacularly high, but its movement clearly comes from the center of the body. In a well-centered dancer you sense that no part of the body is sacrificed for the sake of another. For instance, if the leg is high, the chest and back don't buckle, one side of the rib cage doesn't look shorter than the other, and in general there's no distortion of the body. In essence, finding your center allows you to put gravity to work for you. By learning to sense the movement of all body parts from your center, you never lose track of any of them and they stay in balance with each other.

Finding your center really depends on good placement, and when you work on achieving one, you work on the other at the same time. You'll find that the less distorted your body is when it works, the more you put the natural fact of gravity to use, and the fewer times you force your muscles and joints to operate against their inclination, the better you'll dance and the less you'll be prone to injury.

WARMING UP

Dance classes always begin with a series of warm-up exercises. These are small, localized movement sequences that prepare you for larger and more expansive dancing as the class progresses. In tap class you'll do plain brushes and flaps, for instance, before you go into more complex and faster combinations of steps. In jazz class you'll do a standing and/or a sitting warm-up, working on different parts of your body one at a time, before you do full-scale kicks, leaps, and turns. Modern dance classes similarly have a sitting and/or a standing warm-up, and in ballet class the warm-up is usually done standing at the barre.

If you were to try big, full-scale movement without a warm-up, you could do serious damage to yourself. Basically, the purpose of the in-class warm-up is to ready you for movement that requires more and deeper involvement of the body so that you'll be able to do it without stress and strain.

In many instances you can warm up simply by doing the exercises the teacher conducts during the first part of the class. But as individuals we all have special needs for getting ready to move. Some of us have tensions in certain areas—like our necks and shoulders—or we have joints that need to be loosened up more than the regular in-class warm-up will allow. To take account of these individual needs, and to avoid stressing or straining those of your muscles and joints which you've found by experience need a little extra warming up, you should plan to arrive for class in time to have a five- to ten-minute personalized pre-class warm-up.

Keep in mind that this should be very gentle and non-strenuous and should be designed to loosen you up. Although some dancers may work differently, any serious muscle-building or extended stretching exercises that are part of your personalized development program are generally better done after class than before.

Here are some suggestions for a pre-class warm-up. Follow those you think apply to your particular needs:

- *To loosen your neck and upper back muscles:* Sit on the floor in tailor or Indian fashion, legs crossed, arms hanging easily at your sides, palms down on the floor. Roll your head smoothly from side to side a few times. Then roll it all the way around a few times, gently and easily. (You can keep your eyes closed while you're doing this.)
- *To loosen your shoulders:* Sit in tailor or Indian fashion, arms easily at your sides, palms down on the floor. Raise your shoulders to your ears, then let them drop freely. Repeat a few times. Next, roll your shoulders in gentle, easy forward circles, then in backward

ones. Finally, raise one arm to the front, then over-head, then down to the back, smoothly and easily. Repeat several times with each arm, then with both together.

● *To lengthen your lower back:* Sit with the soles of your feet together, knees dropped out to the sides, hands resting on the ankles. Let your breath out as you gently relax forward, dropping your head over your feet. Stay there, breathing in and out gently, and feel your lower back lengthening. Return gently to a straight sitting position. Repeat several times.

● *To loosen your hip joints:* Sit with the soles of your feet together, knees dropped out to the sides, hands resting on your ankles. Very gently bounce your knees up and down. Concentrate on feeling an opening of your hip joints.

● *To lengthen the hamstring muscles in the backs of your thighs:* Lie on the floor, face up, arms resting at your sides, soles of your feet on the floor and knees bent up and together. Straighten one leg with toes directed as straight up toward the ceiling as they'll easily go. Alternate legs a few times. Then straighten one leg, place your hands in back of your knee, and gently pull your leg in toward your chest. Repeat a few times, alternating legs. (Incidentally, you should keep the soles of your feet on the floor and knees bent whenever you're lying face up; it protects the small of your back.) Next, sit with your legs out straight in front of you. Drop your body over your legs. Remain there for about thirty seconds, breathing in and out gently. Don't force your body over, just hang.

As you learn more about what your special warm-up needs are, you'll add to this basic routine. You may also add to it when you encounter teachers who expect you to warm yourself up quite substantially before class begins so that you can go more quickly into more complex movement. A more extensive pre-class routine is a good idea during cold weather, too, because it takes longer to warm up your muscles then.

WARMING DOWN

Your pre-class personalized warm-up will ready you for movement, but you also need something to slow your body down after class. Being gentle about asking your body to make transitions from one type of activity to another helps reduce stress and strain, whether it's in changing from quiet to strenuous movement or vice versa.

In almost every dance class the teacher gives a final exercise sequence or activity that's designed to warm you down; some easy stretches or pliés are common. These end-of-class rituals do serve to quiet your body's engine, but not every class has them, and in any case you may want to add your own personal warming-down routine.

I've found one simple way that works is to take my time about dressing after class. I try to arrange my schedule so that I don't have to make a mad dash from class to another appointment. I allow ample time to calm my muscles and nerves, to dry off, and to generally come down from my revved-up level. If I know that staying until the end of class will mean a rush to be on time for something that follows, I'll leave class a few minutes early so that I'll have at least some warm-down time.

Of course, individual needs vary, and you may be the kind of person who thrives on bopping nonstop from one activity to the next. Keep your mind open to the possibility that a warm-down might help even you to adjust more easily from class to your next activities.

NERVES

The action of your muscles depends on the operation of your nerves. Without nervous impulses you could never move. Essential as nerves are in this sense, they can work to your disadvantage when they're overactive and cause you to be tense.

Nervousness and its resulting muscular tension can be brought on by many things, anxiety, fear, and worry being the foremost causes. Dancers are often anxious about their careers, afraid of not "making it," worried about the development of their technique. Any dance student also may have fears and worries about events or problems in the rest of his or her life.

Ironically, it's nervous tension that can induce the very events a person fears. Tension constricts blood vessels, thereby hurting circulation when you most need it to nourish the body's cells. It inhibits free respiration, thereby cutting down the exchange of fresh oxygen for the waste products the body needs to rid itself of. It makes muscles tighten or contract when you most need them to be flexible and relaxed, and coordination to be spastic when you most urgently want it to be smooth.

Nervous tension puts the body under stress because it doesn't allow efficient operation. To be efficient, muscles must be able to relax freely in between contractions. It is only from their resting length that they obtain maximum use from succeeding nervous impulses to contract. Excessive tension also keeps all the systems of the body in an unnaturally alert state, not giving them a chance to slow down and rest from their chores.

Stage fright is a kind of nervousness that affects almost every performer, and occasionally dance students experience it even though they're in class and not about to go on the stage. For performance, it can work to your advantage, giving you that extra spurt of adrenalin you need. It usually dissipates after you've been on stage a few minutes, anyway, and leaves you to enjoy your dancing. In class, though, continued nervousness doesn't help you. You may sometimes feel it when you're trying a new class or when the teacher gives a combination of steps that looks impossible to do. Perhaps its roots lie in that deep, dark fear we all have of making fools of ourselves. Will everyone think you can't dance? Maybe they'll think you're dumb. Will they snicker?

Of course, the fear that underlies these thoughts is irrational, and the causes may remain unconscious. Nonetheless, you should be aware that nervousness affects your dancing and can put stresses and strains on your body. The best thing to do when you're nervous is some deep breathing. Try to clear your head and calm down. If you continue to feel jittery, don't overtax yourself on the next step or exercise. Go easy until you feel the nervousness pass and know you're in better control of yourself.

Nerves are an extremely personal thing; their function is based in your nature, the people and events you've been exposed to since infancy, the foods you eat, the sleep you get, and your everyday activities. Each person has to find the right formula for minimizing nervous tension. More important, though, is to be aware that it can be disturbing to your dancing. Don't have the same expectations of yourself when you're nervous as when you're chugging along calmly. Take it a little easier.

CLASSES, CLASSES, AND MORE CLASSES

I once overheard a dancer say she was on her way to her fourth ballet class of the day. I don't know if she made it, but I certainly wondered whether it would do her any good if she did. Each person has a different capacity for work and an individual approach to learning, but four classes a day would seem to put anyone under a bit too much stress. Generally, it's important to keep in touch with what's useful to your own development. Don't jump on the class bandwagon just because everyone else seems to. Be sure that the number of classes you take is really right for you.

I can't tell you exactly what your personal needs will be for the frequency of your classes, but I can give you some general guidelines. These should help you set a basic minimum and an ultimate maximum for yourself.

Body composition. One element in the number of classes you should take is your general body tone. If you tend toward a looser, softer type of muscle, you may find you need class more often to remain strong and centered than if you're sinewy and tight. If you tend to be very tight, however, you may need class more often to keep your body stretched out. Also along the lines of basic equipment is your alignment. If that's generally fairly good, you'll need fewer classes to maintain it. If your skeleton tends to get out of kilter easily, you'll need class more frequently.

General physical condition. Daily variations in your general condition will also affect your capacity for class. For example, if you're exhausted you can do yourself more harm than good by taking class, because injuries are more likely to occur at times when you're tired. You are also simply not getting your money's worth. If a snack, a nap, or some relaxing doesn't revive you before class, you'll probably want to skip it.

A severe cold or the onset of illness may also be indicators of less-than-optimum conditions for dancing. Sometimes a class will help you "sweat out" a cold that's threatening. But it may make things worse if an illness has taken a firm hold. I once went to a rehearsal with a fever; it did nothing for my dancing or my health, and I don't recommend it to anyone.

Special developmental needs. Different individuals will always have different developmental needs. One dancer may have to work for more strength, another for more stretch, a third for more breath and relaxation in movement. To account for your body's special needs, you may wish to add a class or two to your regular routine so that you can work on the particular area in which you need development. Some schools offer special classes—in stretch, for example—and certain techniques inherently address what you may be after—ballet builds strength, and Hawkins technique builds flow. You can add one or two of these classes, or, as an alternative, you might take them in place of one or two of the classes you normally go to each week.

Objectives. If you want to dance professionally, you should take class daily. And after you've reached your professional goal, you'll continue with daily classes to maintain your technique.

Students who dance for fitness or as a form of recreation need classes on a regular basis too, though not daily. You should plan on a minimum of one class a week, though two or three would be better. If you don't attend class regularly you can put stresses and strains on your body when you do take class. It's also no fun to reach a certain level, drop back a few notches, and then have to start crawling back up again.

Working deeply. When you've reached the intermediate level you should begin to give some serious thought to how you work in class. You'll have had enough experience with your body to differentiate the sensations of working deeply from those of working superficially. If you can get closely in touch with the feeling and the process you go through to reach the point where you're working deeply, you can derive much more from each class you take. Then, by taking fewer classes but working deeply in each one, you'll be able to eliminate the stresses and strains that several daily classes might impose on you.

Everyone probably has a special way of describing it, but for me the sensation of working deeply means operating from the very core of my joints. They feel fluid and efficient, like clean, well-oiled, shiny stainless-steel machinery. My muscles feel supple and warm, stretchy and elastic, and they seem to perform effortlessly. When I'm working deeply I never find myself holding my breath or fighting for movement. Everything seems to "go" or "happen," with my mental concentration integrated into the total experience of the movement. This description may sound a little mystical; in a way, when you work deeply, you do transcend yourself.

DANCING FULL OUT

Once you warm up properly and learn to work deeply, you won't have far to go to dance "full out"—an expression that's used to describe dancing that's done to its maximum and that sometimes will take your breath away if you're watching.

Every dance class, whether in ballet, modern, jazz, or tap, progresses from small warm-up exercises to those requiring use of your body in large movement that covers space. In the smaller, warm-up exercises, working correctly means that you'll concentrate on such aspects as placement and contact with your bodily sensations. You may also put some of your attention into analyzing a technical problem. But when it comes time for the larger, dancier movements in the second half of class or across the floor, it's essential to practice dancing full out.

You should dance full out on a regular basis, too. If you do it only every now and then, your intermittent attempts may strain your body and possibly cause an injury.

It's important to dance full out also because you don't want to lock yourself into an analytical type of dancing, where you pick apart the technical details of every finger and toe that you move. An important ingredient in learning to dance is to just do the movement—to become totally involved without intellectual review, letting go of any inspection that would stop the movement's flow and being conscious perhaps of nothing more than the air whipping across your face. Without this abandon your natural coordination will be stifled, and again the result will be unnecessary stress and strain.

I sometimes encourage myself to dance full out in class by pretending that there's an audience watching. With this idea in mind I seem to move with more clarity, to begin and end each step or gesture more decisively. Being students so much of the time, we can easily forget what it feels like to expand and breathe life into a movement so that it takes on the dimensions of a stage. But that's essentially what it means to dance full out. Although some types of class exercises lend themselves more readily than others to being "performed" in this way, just about anything can be enlarged to performance size. I know for a fact, and you may have noticed yourself, that many choreographers incorporate classroom material into their dances. It isn't so much what a dancer does as how it's done that makes a performance. It may be the simplest of movements—a walk or the tilt of a head—but, done full out, commandingly and with conviction, it can be the most eloquent of gestures.

Dancing full out means that you are involved vigorously and healthily in muscular activity that makes you feel alive and in tune with your body. Your entire being senses participation with full consent; no muscles are overly tense, excessively shortened, or distorted in any way. They are working to capacity, but with enough relaxation in between contractions so that they feel released and free.

Of course, you should never dance full out unless you're fully warmed up; that can be unhealthy for your muscles and joints. You probably won't dance full out in every class you take, either. Your skill in different types of dance, the exercises you do, the types of classes you're in, and your own developmental needs will dictate otherwise. Learning when to dance full out is part of learning to dance. Do things on a less grand scale when you're not warmed up or not feeling up to it or it's not warranted; but don't be timid about giving your all to movement when you're ready for full-blown involvement.

By regularly dancing full out at the opportune times in class, you'll develop a flow and life in your dancing that will serve you well. Not only will it enable you to dance in the truest sense of the word, but it will also prepare your body to accept into its repertoire movement that might otherwise be dangerously taxing.

FORCING

Dancers sometimes mistakenly take a detour off the path of working deeply and dancing full out, and wind up across the border in Force City. The inhabitants here are often grunting and clenching their teeth. They are noticeably holding their breath and have two huge cords protruding on either side of their necks. They are likely to be red in the face, with wrinkled brows and intense expressions.

Sound like anyone you know?

If in class you notice that you've stopped breathing, if the cords in your neck are popping out, and any of the other symptoms I've just described apply, you've started forcing, and it's time for some reevaluation. Your overall alignment may be the problem. Remember that muscles work best when the bones to which they are attached are lined up to permit them maximum use from each contraction. If the bones are not so positioned, you'll have to force to achieve the desired movement.

Or you may not be warming up properly. If you put too much of a load on a muscle or try to stretch it before it's reached optimum temperature, you'll have to force it to do what you want—whether it's to stretch or to contract.

You and your teacher will have to make a joint effort to correct your alignment, improve your approach to warming up, or figure out what's making you force. Whatever you do, don't continue forcing. It stresses and strains your body, can lead to injury, and doesn't produce good dancing.

Dancers who don't force are the most exciting to watch. Baryshnikov, for instance, makes dancing look deliciously easy—like eating ice cream. Other dancers can make you aware of each muscle contraction and each joint's grinding operation, and they're not fun to look at. Even if you're a modern dancer who wants the audience to see how much effort you're using, you shouldn't count on force. To achieve the desired dramatic effects, you need to depend on facility of muscle control. If you develop the habit of forcing in class, your chances of carrying it over to performance are excellent. Watch out for the signs: holding your breath, grunting, clenching your teeth, and so on. Do something about it before you've injured yourself or developed a strained performing quality that you'll have to work on for years to eliminate.

Aches, Pains, and Injuries

MUSCLE SORENESS

Any time you ask your body to do something out of the ordinary, you're likely to experience unusual sensations. In studying dance, because you're trying to develop extraordinary strength and stretch in your muscles, you may become sore from time to time. Even when you've danced regularly for years, if you take a week or two off you'll find your muscles will be sore following your return to your first class.

The physiological basis of muscle soreness isn't exactly clear. Some say it's the accumulation of lactic acid in the muscles, a by-product of muscle contraction. Others say it's tiny tears in the muscles. Whatever the case, it's not a condition you need to worry seriously about.

You can avoid some muscle soreness in several ways: (1) If you take time off from classes (say a week or two), try to do about fifteen minutes of exercises on your own each day. (2) When you go back to your first class, arrive extra early and do a very slow, easy warm-up before class begins. (3) Go home immediately afterward and take a comfortably hot bath; add mineral salts to the water and massage your muscles and joints, staying in the bath for twenty to thirty minutes. Really wallow in it; relax and let go of as much tension as you can. (4) Go back on your regular class schedule; don't stay away because you think your muscles will become more sore from working. Actually, the reverse is true: The exercise you'll get in class will help to stimulate circulation, which will in turn remove waste products (lactic acid) and help repair tissues.

With proper treatment muscle soreness should disappear in two or three days. If it doesn't, you may have strained or pulled a muscle. In general, anything that's minor won't stay with you for more than a week. If you note any symptoms that do, you may need medical attention or, at the very least, rest.

DANGER SIGNS AND INJURIES

If you've been conscientious about working correctly, taking heed of your body's messages, and generally treating it well, you should be able to avoid most of the problems I'm going to talk about in this section. Unfortunately, no one always does everything perfectly, and in the course of a wholehearted dance experiment you may fall victim to an injury. It needn't be incapacitating, though, if you anticipate it and treat it properly and quickly.

Pain. Pain helps you anticipate a potential problem (for instance, when you pull your hand sharply away from a hot stove), and also lets you know that you already have a problem (for example, when you cut yourself). Without pain a person can go right on doing injurious things and never know the difference.

Thus, the reason that pain exists is to alert you to the fact that your body is in trouble. To anyone who says that pain is a natural part of dancing, I say hogwash and nonsense. Pain is your body's way of telling you it is in distress and requires attention and relief.

I am, of course, distinguishing pain from minor discomforts such as muscle soreness. But sometimes dancers grow so accustomed to the throes of physical involvement that they confuse serious pain with minor discomfort and don't pay it any attention at all. To protect yourself against injury, and to hasten your recovery if you do injure yourself, you must stay in touch with the sensation of pain. Don't feel you're a sissy because you recognize that you're feeling pain.

Pain in the ankles, knees, and lower back. If you haven't already done the damage, a good way to anticipate the more common types of dance injuries is to notice any pain whatsoever in your ankles, knees, or lower back. At any time that you feel pain in these joints, *stop whatever you are doing immediately.*

I don't know if emphasizing the words in the last paragraph has made the point sink in. Since I have only the written word available here, I can't shout at you. Let me say it once again: Pain in your knees, ankles, and lower back is simply not to be ignored under any circumstances. Stop whenever you feel it.

The knees and ankles and the small muscles and vertebral joints of the lower back are probably the most frequently injured parts of a dancer's body. It is only through respectful attention to them that you'll enjoy their full, healthy operation throughout your involvement with dancing. Any pain in these areas undoubtedly reflects some way in which you're not working correctly. Have your teacher help you with the problem before it leads to an injury.

In some cases you'll be tempted to ignore pain in your ankles, knees, or back. There won't be any other symptoms of injury—swelling or limited mobility, for instance. And once the joint is warmed up in class, it won't seem to bother you very much. However, ankle, knee, or lower back pain, whether you experience it during or after class, always means there's something wrong. If you continue to work without attending to the situation, you may cause further deterioration of the joint, and, in addition, you may harm other parts of your body.

For instance, if you've done something to your left knee, you may unconsciously and ever so slightly shift a little extra weight onto your right leg. This will strain your right leg. Beyond that, it may set up other compensating mechanisms that will put stress on your other muscles and joints. What started out as a pain in your left knee may end up including a muscle spasm in your neck.

Any time that pain in your ankles, knees, or lower back persists for more than a week, you have two options: (1) rest and (2) see a doctor. You may want to do both.

From this distance I can't diagnose an injury or tell you precisely what's needed to treat it. But I can tell you one thing with absolute certainty: You cannot ignore continued pain in your ankles, knees, or lower back and get away with it for very long. You may in the end commit yourself to a chronic and perhaps incapacitating injury.

Shin splints. Jumping and running, whether in the context of dancing or other physical activity, may cause an aching in the front of your legs from the knee down. Sometimes this ache can be excrutiating. It's called "shin splints."

When you experience shin splints it may mean that you're dancing on concrete. However, it may also mean you're not landing properly when running or jumping. You may not be bending your knees enough or putting your heels down when you land. Or your weight may be held too far back. For the proper muscles to absorb the weight of your body upon landing, you must bend your knees directly over your feet.

Don't continue jumping, leaping, or running in the same way when you experience shin splints. Have your teacher help you figure out what you should do differently to correct the problem. Unless you're dancing on concrete, shin splints are usually a sign that you're working incorrectly. Your work habits may actually be affecting not only your jumps but other aspects of your technique as well.

Immediate versus delayed pain. With some types of injuries or problems you'll experience pain immediately at the time they occur. For example, if you sprain your ankle you'll feel pain at the moment you do it. (The pain may grow worse as the swelling increases later on, but you'll have some when the injury first occurs.)

There's another type of injury in which the pain is delayed; you experience it some time after the injury actually happens. For instance, you may dance through class and feel perfectly fine in the evening and then wake up the next morning with a terrible ache in your back, stabs of pain in your knee, or a sore tendon. The pain in these cases isn't apparent until the next morning, often because swelling hasn't had a chance to occur until then, or because once you stop moving, the injured part stiffens.

Delayed pain sometimes doesn't seem as serious as immediate pain because you may not remember actually doing anything to hurt yourself. You'll tend to think that the pain will disappear just as mysteriously as it arrived. Don't be fooled. Delayed pain can indicate as serious an injury or problem as immediate pain, and you should attend to it with as much care as you would pain in which the cause was apparent.

Treatment. Your first thought in attending to any pain that's immediate, delayed, and/or persistent should be for treatment. Don't be embarrassed about saying you've hurt yourself and need help.

With sprains or potential fractures use ice or cold compresses immediately to keep the swelling down.[16] Any time there's swelling or distortion of a joint, see a doctor and have it X-rayed. Don't make your own diagnosis. If you guess wrong and then follow up with self-prescription, you can shorten or end your dance career. It's true that seeing a doctor costs money, but by seeking treatment immediately after an injury occurs you can save yourself the extended expense of treating a worsened or chronic condition that you initially let go unattended.

It's possible, of course, that you'll never need to see a doctor in an emergency for a dance injury. Just in case you do, though, it's a good idea to prepare in advance and have on hand a list of doctors whom other dancers recommend. Ask around and cross-check the various recommendations. Obtain the names of several doctors, in the event that one or the other is out of town or unable to see you when you need prompt attention. Then, if you do injure yourself, you will at least be secure and perhaps feel a little calmer knowing that you have a capable doctor to turn to.

Recovering from an injury. Who in the world could possibly hate being out of commission more than a dancer? With serious injuries, however, total rest is likely to be the only road to total recovery.

In some cases you can do exercises lying on the floor or those that require minimal involvement of the injured part of your body. Through such exercises you can improve circulation and thereby promote healing. Your doctor will be able to tell you what's best.

The hardest thing will be staying off your feet long enough and letting enough time go by before you try out the healing part to see how it's doing. The next-hardest thing will be keeping up your spirits—not feeling sorry for yourself, mad at yourself, or depressed, and having faith that everything will be all right.

I've had only one injury that put me off my feet for any length of time: an ankle that I sprained so badly I used crutches for a week. I found that dancer friends were among the best people to have around. They could empathize readily, and their talking about dance kept me optimistic. Other friends and family helped too, of course, and were indispensable when it came to groceries, books, and other physical and spiritual necessities.

As a dancer you're likely to be healthier all around than the rest of the population and therefore will heal faster. But, as you probably know, morale can have a serious effect on your recovery. When you're injured, don't forget your emotions and your mental state. Talk to people and do as many things as you can to boost your spirits.

7

The Work Place:
Dealing with
the Physical Environment
of the Dance Studio

New York City, Summer 1966: Small balls of fur waft
across my face as I lie on the floor trying to concentrate on
the teacher's counts. Breathe in, two, three, four; out, two,
three, four; in, two . . . I give up. Some stray hairs have
found their way to my nose, and I blast forth a resounding
sneeze.

An old furrier's loft on Seventh Avenue at Thirtieth Street was
the site of a studio I danced in when I first arrived in New York
to study, during one of the hottest summers on record. After

several classes amid the remains of raccoons and rabbits, I decided the combination of musty smells and odd hairs clinging to my perspiring body was unbearable, and I left for balder parts. The studios I've danced in since have been a lot more pleasant, I'm happy to say.

Due primarily to limited financial resources, dance studios are not always the most finely appointed places. Especially if a teacher is operating independently, the amount of money that's available for studio rental won't be very great. As a result the facilities will leave much to be desired (for example, only cold running water in the bathroom, a tiny dressing room, peeling walls and ceilings). The neighborhood location may not be very safe or easily accessible, either. If you find an exceptional teacher, however, it sometimes is worth the discomfort of the studio and the inconvenient location. I would have danced in a dungeon and gone as far as Hoboken to take class with the late James Waring, and sometimes it felt as if I did both. His studio looked out on a dismal air shaft and was located on a deserted street in lower Manhattan. But I learned things from Jimmy that are with me to this day, and that I don't think I could have learned from anyone else.

You have to weigh the trade-offs. If it takes you an hour each way to reach your teacher, the wear and tear on you may seriously affect the amount of energy you have left for dancing. Or if your favorite teacher operates in a studio where the floors are so slippery that you worry about falling more than you dance, you may also have to take stock of the situation.

Studios that are better financed will usually provide a more-than-adequate setup. The larger schools, for example, which in some cases have a benefactor, may offer the student near-perfect dance conditions. The same is true of many colleges, where tuition and other funds are designated for use by the dance department. In such places both the studio and the performing facilities can be quite sumptuous, with full-size dressing rooms that have professional make-up mirrors and showers.

Whatever place you have chosen to study in, whether it's a converted ballroom, a basketball court, the front parlor of an apartment, a sometime art gallery, a former dress-manufacturing loft, or a specially designed and super-deluxe dance studio, there will always be environmental conditions to take into account for your dancing. Some may present obstacles you'll have to overcome; others will be standard features you should know how to use to your advantage (for instance, the barre and the mirror). This chapter gives you some insight into making the best of your physical surroundings in dance classes.

Studio Size

TOO MANY STUDENTS FOR THE SPACE

One of the factors that can make a studio too small is the number of students dancing in it at any given time. When there are too many, making it crowded, your dancing is likely to shrink. Some teachers are alert to spacing problems and seem to have an instinct for placing and grouping students so that everyone feels there's room to move. Some concentrate more on other aspects of teaching, and leave you to fend for yourself.

If you get the feeling that your dancing is cramped because the studio is too small for all the people in it, and that the spacing arrangements made by the teacher are too casual to consistently give you enough room to dance, you'll want to figure out how you can improve the situation. You might try speaking to the teacher. Or look around more carefully on your own. Is there a space you haven't considered using, perhaps because it's not directly in front of the mirror? It might be better to trade off seeing yourself in the mirror for more room to move.

Another possible attack on the space problem is through accommodating steps. For example, suppose you're repeating a series of steps that travels forward. In between each repetition, if the music allows, take an accommodating step backward to give yourself more room for the next time you move forward. Or suppose you're doing a series that combines small and large steps. You can do the small steps very small so that you have more space when you come to the larger steps. In a series that has steps moving in opposite directions, try to move equally in both directions so that you finish in the place where you began.

Arriving at class a little earlier and being generally assertive about claiming your ground may also help fill your need for space. By arriving early you'll have a wider choice of places, and by claiming your space in no uncertain terms you'll avoid being eased out of it by anyone else. Do whatever is needed to make it absolutely clear that you own a space and do not intend to be inched off.

There's one teacher I've taken class with in New York City, however, in whose studio none of this makes any difference. The studio is large by ordinary standards, but so many students occupy it that in the four classes I took there I felt I was engaged in an unending battle for a handkerchief-size plot of floor and a cubic foot or two of breathable air. The teacher has an excellent reputation, and many fine dancers study with her, but I found the space conditions impossible to live with.

Many popular teachers give more than one level of class and often conduct two classes a day (one at each level). Frequently the more advanced class will be the less crowded one. If you have doubts about your ability to handle the advanced class, but feel your dancing is suffering because of space constraints in the slower class, talk to the teacher. Perhaps you'll jointly decide you should give the advanced class a try.

STUDIOS THAT ARE BASICALLY SMALL

There are studios that, while they may be large enough for the number of students in them, are too small for very broad, expansive traveling movement. The limited square footage of the room may prevent you from bursting out and sailing forth across the space, even when the dance steps you're doing seem to call for it.

In a small studio the ceiling can also be a problem. Ceiling height makes a difference in your dancing, just as it does in your everyday existence. Your experience of entering a room with a low ceiling is generally different from that when you walk into a high-ceilinged room. Male dancers who are tall and at the same time high jumpers also run the risk of swiping a low ceiling. For most of us, though, the difference is more psychological than physical. The effect of a low ceiling is to make your dancing smaller.

If your favorite teacher's studio consists of a small room with low ceilings, your dancing will develop to reflect these conditions. You can learn to adjust, but to stay in touch with the big movements that are an important part of dancing, it's necessary to work in open terrain. If most of your dancing is done in tight quarters, take a class every once in a while in a studio where the expanse of floor leaves you breathless. Then let go and enjoy yourself.

SPACES THAT ARE TOO LARGE

So far I've talked only about places that don't give you enough room for your dancing. But there are also some spaces that can be too big. I took my first dance classes at college in a gymnasium that felt like a coliseum. Even though the teacher herded us all into a fairly small corner, once we moved out of it we began to feel a little lost.

Too much empty space around you can dissipate your energies and dwarf your sense of yourself. If you find you're floundering in a gigantic area, try sidling up to your classmates. Besides helping define the space around you, they'll exude energy that you'll be able to pick up and apply in your own movement. You'll emanate reciprocal energy that neighboring students will be able to put to use in their dancing.

Incidentally, on stage your space is defined by the lighting as well as by physical dimensions. The space you perform in can be shrunk to the right size for the dance you're doing by the way the lights are hung and projected. As a performer you must learn to adapt to many different theaters and types of lighting, and often you must do so quickly because you'll have only a limited number of rehearsals on stage. Adapting to the size of studios will give you experience you can apply to your on-stage work.

Floors

Adaptable as most dancers are, if there's anything that can send them into a flap, it's a floor that's tough to dance on. Floors can be too slippery, too sticky, or too hard. They may be uneven, with warped boards or curling linoleum tiles; in some cases the entire floor may slope, sag, and undulate. Another element in floor conditions is the weather. On hot, humid days you'll feel as though you can't separate your feet from the floor. On cool, dry days you'll practically skate on the very same floor.

Although most dance schools and teachers do their best to provide a good floor, many miss the mark. Here are some suggestions for adjusting to floor conditions that might make you otherwise miserable.

SLIPPERINESS

Slick floors in the ballet studio are traditionally treated with rosin. Usually you'll find a "rosin box" or a special corner of the studio where you can get some to put on your shoes. Most dancers dip their toes and heels into it or else tramp through the box briefly. The trick in using rosin on your ballet shoes is getting enough but not too much for the dancing you're about to perform. For leaps and runs the more you have on, the better. For turns, though, in which you pivot on one foot, you don't want to create so much resistance that you won't be able to get around.

To preserve the surface of some floors, you may not be allowed to use rosin at all, even if you're taking ballet or jazz classes where you need the extra friction. Under these circumstances, if the floor is slippery the best solution may be to work in your bare feet. If you prefer to keep your shoes on, you can try dampening the soles. Put a small puddle of water in an out-of-the-way corner and dip your feet into it. Allow a minute or two for the water to soak in before you start dancing. You can return to the puddle every so often during class to keep your shoes moist enough to create the right amount of friction between you and the floor. Be careful not to get the shoes sopping, however; this can make slippery conditions even worse.

There are few floors that will be too slippery for bare feet. If you are faced with one, though, see if there's any rosin around and ask the teacher if it's allowed on the floor you're dancing on. Then use just a tiny amount on the bottoms of your feet. If you use too much, you'll create havoc with the skin on your soles.

In tap class you won't always have rosin to fall back on. Some tap studios just don't use it. If you've put treaded no-slip rubber soles on your shoes, they'll help prevent slipping.

Generally, whenever a floor is slippery you'll have a better chance of remaining upright if you concentrate on keeping your weight over your toes and off your heels. Should you start to fall, you can catch yourself more easily if your weight is lurching forward than if it's careening back.

STICKINESS

Although it's more common for ballet dancers to look for greater rather than less friction, floors can sometimes offer too much resistance when they become heavily rosined. If that's the case, you should avoid the rosin box. Don't go to it purely out of habit. Also take into account that turns require more force when you're working on a sticky floor, and your timing and coordination can be upset if you're not accustomed to it. When you find yourself fighting to get around because the floor is resisting too much, you may want to consider using less force even though the result may be a single rather than a double turn. If you develop the habit of throwing yourself forcefully into a turn, you may have a hard time adjusting when you dance on a less resistant floor.

Any time bare feet meet too much resistance you're liable to open "splits" in the bottoms of your feet. These are fissures or deep cracks in the toughened areas of the sole (usually at the ball of the foot) that expose the tender layer of skin beneath. They take a long time to heal and are annoying and painful.

To avoid splits on sticky floors, some dancers tape their feet with white adhesive, wrapping it around at the ball of the foot and across the metatarsals at the top to keep the tape in place. Wearing socks also will help you avoid too much friction. Many ballet dancers who don't like to wear shoes for the warm-up at the barre wear socks instead so that their feet will slide properly as required. You can wear them for the warm-up in modern class as well, if you find your feet sticking to the floor at inopportune times. Remember, though, to take them off once you start moving from your spot.

Another solution for sticky floors and bare feet is talcum powder. Dust a very small amount on the balls of your feet. Be careful not to overdo it—too much can make the floor too slick.

IRREGULARLY SURFACED FLOORS

Depending on what they're used for besides ballet classes and how well they're maintained, some floors become an irregular and unpredictable combination of slippery, sticky, and just right. The same studio may serve for both ballet and modern classes, for instance, rosin being used for ballet and cleaned off the floor for modern. The cleanup usually leaves some spots smoother than others, with the result that there's no consistent surface you can depend on. Floors that are not swept and washed often or well enough will suffer the same fate.

When you notice a slippery spot in a ballet or jazz class, if rosin is available, put some on your shoes and walk back and forth across it. If there's no rosin you can, instead, sprinkle some water lightly on it, but I'd check with the teacher before doing so. The floor might be a type that doesn't respond to water. It's also a good idea to alert the teacher to any seriously slick spots in the studio. That way everyone in class can be warned to avoid them.

To fix a sticky spot, it's usually necessary to wash it, and you might not be interested in going down on your hands and knees to do the job. You might let the teacher know it's there, though.

Places near a rosin box or corner are generally much stickier than the rest of the studio floor. As students troop in and out of the box, a residue builds up around it, creating a rough surface where you'll encounter too much friction for almost any dancing. Don't dance too close to the rosin box if you can help it.

UNEVEN FLOORS

It would be nice if slickness and stickiness were the only floor conditions you had to watch out for. They're certainly enough to keep you occupied. Unfortunately, there are more problems you may have to contend with.

As wood and linoleum-tile floors grow old and worn, the edges of some of the pieces that form them may start to come up above the level of the surrounding pieces. In older buildings the entire floor may tilt toward one side, giving you the feeling of going uphill and downhill as you dance back and forth. Wavy floors also exist in some dance studios. They may give you pause as you're dancing, since the floor may not be as high or low as you expect it to be in different places.

All of these conditions are usually not absolutely impossible to work with, but they will affect your dancing. You can accustom yourself to almost any of them, learning what places to avoid and when to anticipate problems. If you perform, this experience can prepare you for stage floors, which often are not the smooth, regular surfaces, you would have them be. Unless you think the floor in class is dangerous (you can discuss this with the teacher), it's probably not a bad idea to try to figure out how to work successfully with it. If you do find it lethal, consider switching the place you're studying in.

RESILIENCE

The best type of floor for dancing is a wood-based, resilient one. Many dance studios have them. Some, however, have wood surfaces only, with an underlying layer of concrete. As you probably know from pounding pavement, concrete is not resilient. It doesn't "give" as you put your weight into it.

Of all the difficult-to-work-on floors, I consider the concrete-based one the worst. I think it is also potentially the most dangerous. The damage it does to your body is insidious, developing slowly over time while you're unaware it's happening. When a floor isn't resilient, your joints and muscles receive a shock each time you land on it or run across it. Unlike wood, which absorbs your weight and bounces it back off the floor, acting like a cushion, concrete just doesn't respond. The entire impact of your weight when landing must be taken in your joints—your ankles, knees, hips, and back.

If you can possibly avoid it, never dance on a concrete-based floor. If there are any doubts in your mind about the floor you're dancing on, and you find your joints and shins aching a great deal, ask whether there's any concrete hidden under the surface. For those times when it's absolutely necessary for you to dance on a nonresilient floor (sometimes this happens when you must perform in a specific theater), don't jump as high (during rehearsals) as you would on a good floor. In fact, try not to jump at all.

Pillars and Posts

Depending on a building's vintage, the absence of steel beams in its construction may leave you with the problem of supporting pillars and posts dotted here and there across the dance floor. It will, of course, be obvious that you'll want to avoid running into these, but that may be harder than you think.

Pillars and posts sometimes act like magnets, pulling you toward them. The reason is that they stand out from the "landscape" of the rest of the room, catching your eye and pulling your body in their direction. This is the same principle that applies when you "spot" a turn. Your eyes focus strongly on an object or spot, and your body turns in its direction. When you're traveling across space, whether it's in a straight or a turning pattern, unless your spot is very decisive, a pillar or post can distract you and pull you toward it rather than your intended spot.

The best way to work in a room with pillars and posts is to keep your focus and your sense of center very strong. Clearly see what you're looking at, and deeply feel where your body center is in space. These habits will serve you well whether you're dancing around pillars and posts or on the grandest stage in the world.

Temperature

Most dancers love heat and hate cold. Cold means discomfort and potential injury. Heat means supple, stretchy muscles and deliciously loose joints. Unfortunately, we can't always dance in warm climates, and the winters can force us to work under frigid conditions.

Heating systems vary in their efficiency, and so do landlords in their generosity. As a result the studio you dance in may be very cold in the winter. If you feel at all chilly at any time you're dancing, you should put on something to keep warm. Use whatever woolen tights, sweaters, or body suits you need to cover yourself up. Find ones that won't constrict your movement, and make sure they're loose enough to allow good circulation. Follow the other guidelines for dress mentioned in Chapter 4.

Occasionally you'll run across a dance studio that's air-conditioned for hot summer days. Unless air conditioning is very subtle, it can harm your body. While air conditioning eliminates those rivers of sweat that would otherwise pour from your body on humid ninety-nine-degree days, the risk of injury may outweigh this one advantage. If you dance in any studios where the air conditioning is more than mild, wear warm-up clothing.

The Barre

The barre and ballet have gone together for ages, and it's still true today that just about every ballet class begins with exercises that you do standing alongside and holding on to a barre.

In its beginning modern dance freed itself from many of ballet's constraints, including the barre, and the tradition grew of starting classes in the center of the floor, either sitting or standing. Today, however, you'll find modern dance classes that start at the barre and some ballet classes that start in the center of the studio. With the increasing number of dance teachers, more and more ideas about training are being put into practice, and it's not possible to say exactly what place the barre will play in the dance classes you elect to take. But whatever the class, if a barre is involved you should know why it's there and how to use it to your advantage.

There are four basic uses for the barre: (1) to help you place your body *parts* correctly for dancing; (2) to help you place your body *weight* correctly for dancing; (3) to lend support until you build enough strength in or warm up the muscles you will use for dancing; and (4) for stretching and other exercises in which you need something to put your leg on or to hang on to. The first two uses of the barre are to help you gain placement: alignment of individual body parts and the placement of your total body weight. Placement forms the foundation upon which your dance technique is built by giving you the sense of center that makes your dancing solid and consistent.

Alignment of just a single body part can be a serious determining factor in your technical abilities. Take your head, for example. It weighs between ten and twelve pounds. This is a large mass to set down on top of the long, relatively narrow column that is your spine. To complicate matters, this great lump, useful as it may be, has the ability to twist and turn, bob up and down, rock to and fro, and tilt from side to side. This is no problem when you're doing ordinary things. In fact, it's quite an advantage to have such mobility. Unless your head is resting properly, however, it can be a serious disadvantage to your dancing. It can make all the difference between whether you balance or not. It can prevent you from changing directions quickly. It can enable you to turn or prevent you from turning, regardless of how strong or "placed" you might otherwise be. On a par with the alignment of your head is the alignment of your pelvis. The way it tips or tilts can either devastate your dancing or make it exquisite.

It would be wonderful if we were all born with and could maintain the kind of placement that's needed for dancing. We're not, however, and although some of us naturally have better placement than others, we all must work for it.

A barre helps by providing a consistent, external cue for your visual and kinesthetic senses. Visually, as you work at the barre over time, you'll begin to absorb a sense of the distance between your body and the barre. Kinesthetically, you'll begin to recognize how your muscles feel when your body is properly placed in relation to it. You can readily come back to this relationship because of the connection between your "muscle memory" and peripheral environmental cues. (If you've ever had the experience of driving an automatic-shift after a standard-shift car, you'll be familiar with the phenomenon of muscle memory. You don't need to shift an automatic car, but your muscles do it anyway, because that's what they remember to do when you're sitting in the driver's seat.)

When you stand at a barre to work in class, you should put your hand slightly in front of your body, never directly beside it or behind it. By placing it in front of you, you help keep the expanse of your back wide, which is the best condition for your dancing. You should feel breadth across your back and between your shoulder blades, and a continuity of line stretching from the arm that is extended away from the barre across to the one on the barre. A good way to find the right place for your hand on the barre is to use both arms rather than one for the port-de-bras (arm movement) that begins each barre exercise. If you've done the port-de-bras correctly, the arm that's next to the barre will be far enough in front of you. All you need to do then is to lower your hand to it.

You may also need to reposition your hand as you work in different exercises. For instance, if you lunge forward onto your leg, you must move the hand that's on the barre forward, too. If you lunge backward, you move it back. Always try to keep it in approximately the same relationship to your torso.

Some ballet teachers will tell you to drop your elbow once you've put your hand on the barre. Others will tell you to keep it raised. Follow whichever method your teacher prescribes.

Many teachers like to have you use the barre as lightly as you possibly can. They believe that the barre is there only to rest your hand on and relate to in space. They will tell you never to grab it or hang on to it, reasoning that since you're obviously not meant to use the barre when you're performing on stage or dancing in the center of the floor, you shouldn't be dependent on it. Here again, though, there are differences of opinion. Many other teachers feel that you need to hold on to the barre quite firmly at times to help you get centered or for specific exercises or until the right muscles are strong enough or warmed up enough to be used correctly. The barre gives you that little extra something you need to feel substantial, and these teachers say that you can develop the wrong muscles or injure yourself if you don't use the barre for that bit of help. Your independence from the barre, they feel, develops because you make use of it when you need to.

You should follow whichever practice your teacher suggests, but if you do use the barre firmly for support at times, try not to distort the shape of your arm, shoulder, or back. Try to remember to press down on the barre rather than to pull from it.

In doing stretches at the barre, a general guideline is to retain the proper placement of your body weight and its parts while you are isolating the part to be stretched. If you are isolating your right leg, for example, be sure your right hip is not higher than the left, that you are not crunching your rib cage on one side or the other, and that the foot you are standing on is lined up directly beneath the knee. Be alert to pain in the knees, ankles, and lower back when you do barre stretches. It's easy to slip into poor placement and to put undue strain on these areas.

For any other exercises in which you are specifically instructed to put some part of you or your weight on the barre, again remember to maintain good placement and not to use excessive force. It's very easy to injure yourself otherwise.

The one use I haven't listed for the barre is as a place to rest between exercises. It's a very inviting spot to drop your elbows over and hang from, and I must confess to giving in on days when I'm particularly tired or frazzled. But doing so tends to raise your shoulders and distort your chest and back. It's a good idea to keep your weight evenly distributed over your two feet and to stand up comfortably straight all the time you're in class. It keeps your muscles ready for action and your mind alert for what comes next.

WITHOUT THE BARRE

In spite of the advantages of using a barre, it is possible, and for some techniques preferable, to train without it. You learn to find your placement and your center, and to build the right muscles without any extraneous aids, and obviously this transfers quite readily to any performing you do on a stage. Another advantage to not using a barre is that it makes you free to do warm-up combinations that travel a bit in space, and in which you can go from side to side or backward and forward with greater latitude than when you are stuck at a barre.

When a barre isn't used in a class, you may do some of your placement work while sitting or lying on the floor. Using the floor can be, in a way, like using the barre. You'll develop an awareness of your body weight and the alignment of its parts in relation to the floor rather than the barre, but it will serve you in a similar way.

You'll also use the floor to stretch on. As you would when doing stretches at the barre, you should keep your body parts aligned, watch out for pain in your joints, and avoid using excessive force.

When dancers do their pre-class warm-ups, they have different preferences for using or going without the barre. In my case, since my initial dance training was in ballet with a barre, I feel I need to begin any dancing I do by resting my hand on it or on some similar object. Perhaps it's psychological, but I feel it helps me warm up more correctly. When I take a class in which I know I won't be using a barre (whether it's modern, jazz, or tap), I do part of my personal warm-up with my hand on the piano or a water pipe or any object that will serve the purpose of a barre. After I've warmed up this way and I've established a feeling of my center, I'm fine for the rest of the class. If you've trained with a barre, you may find the same will work for you in classes where it isn't used.

TWO KINDS OF BARRES

As an aside, the term "barre" is used to refer both to the long pole or pipe that you put your hand on as well as to the series of exercises you do at the beginning of a dance class. That's why dancers sometimes say "I'm taking just the barre today," meaning that they're going to stay only for the part of class in which the warm-up exercises are done. Some modern dancers also will talk about "taking the barre" in their modern classes, even when there's no sign of the actual physical object in the studio.

Mirrors

Some time ago one of the teachers I was studying with moved to a new studio where the mirrors hadn't yet been installed. Trying to take class in the new place was like coming into a dark room from brilliant sunlight. Several classes went by before I stopped falling off my feet and wobbling in my knees, but during that time I learned a valuable lesson: You can grow to depend on the mirror for the wrong things.

The mirror serves two main purposes in a dance studio: (1) It creates the feeling of space, opening the front of the room to infinity instead of leaving the wall as a dead end to abruptly stop your focus and your movement flow. The mirror makes it possible for you to look beyond, helping to open your face and keep it alive. It makes you feel as though you might move fully in its direction. By doing these things, it helps you to achieve clear, extended lines with your body. (2) The mirror can also be used to check on alignment and other aspects of technique. You can see, for example, if one hip is higher than the other when it's not supposed to be or if your foot is really pointed or your lower back kept as long as it should be.

The first purpose of the mirror in a dance studio is the more important of the two. But in our efforts to learn and improve, we sometimes reverse the order. Instead of an open face and long lines, we achieve a furrowed look as we spy on our reflection, checking each move we make to see what faults or perfection we may discern.

If you're working on something that requires you to check

yourself in the mirror, do so only as often as is absolutely necessary. When you note that you've achieved what you're after, look beyond your reflection and try to *feel it on the inside*. In other words, don't stop at the outward reflection. You may become overly dependent on it for cues that should really take the form of sensations within your body. What you see in the mirror is only a reflection of the real you. Your flesh-and-blood self is something else, and you want to keep in touch with that living, breathing being—not with the illusory image in the mirror.

It's a good idea to measure your mirror dependency every once in a while by working in a place in the studio where you can't see your reflection. You may be astounded and delighted with all the sensations you've been missing.

Dressing Rooms, Bathrooms, and General Conditions

There are two ways you can travel in Europe: in minimum-rate rooms with a shared bath down the hall or in better accommodations with a private bath in your room. If you're a private-bath-only type of person, you may not be happy with the dressing and bath facilities and the overall conditions of some studios. At times they are barely adequate, and usually they're very far from luxurious.

I must give credit to the teachers I've studied with for doing all in their power to keep their studios clean, neat, and supplied with the needed paper and soap. But sometimes the basic equipment and space just aren't there, despite any teacher's best efforts.

You'll have to weigh the advantages against the obstacles. Are spanking-clean, spacious, and beautiful surroundings absolutely critical to your dancing and on a par with quality of teaching?

Then you'll want to search out a studio where both are coordinated. (Good luck!) If you're willing to put up with less in the way of surroundings for the sake of good teaching, however, a run-down studio can grow to be totally insignificant.

If you're so inclined, you might help improve conditions. You might bring hangers for the dressing room or donate an old chair or paper-towel dispenser. You might join a weekend paint party to freshen the walls, or liven a corner with one of your house plants. Check with your teacher to see if there's something you can do.

Smooth Sailing: Policies and Practices for Navigating in the Dance Studio

Public places often post notices about the behavior required in them: NO SMOKING, ENTER HERE, FORM SINGLE LINE, EXPRESS CHECKOUT—CUSTOMERS WITH NO MORE THAN TEN ITEMS. Rules and regulations make it possible for people to be together without getting in each other's way, without creating hazards for each other, and without interfering in each other's purpose for being there.

You won't find too many signs posted in a dance studio; NO SMOKING, maybe. But there are some very specific, often unspoken, policies and practices to know about that are essential for order and safety and for any learning to occur in the studio.

As you read through this chapter, you'll find many suggestions that will sound like good common sense and that will seem very obvious to anyone with a head on his shoulders. There'll also be suggestions that you have probably put into practice already if you've taken class for any length of time. In these cases the recommendations I'll make will reinforce what you already know. Be on the lookout, though, for items that may be new to you—especially if you're just beginning to study.

Unfortunately, rules and regulations and policies and procedures always seem to come out sounding a little harsh and unfriendly. Don't be put off by the tone or offended by the directness of some of the suggestions in this chapter. They're meant only to inform and advise you, and to make class a productive experience for everyone.

Claiming Your Ground

Recently I was on a Los Angeles freeway at rush hour, alternately crawling and speeding dangerously along in the midst of thousands of cars all trying to make use of the same road. I thought to myself, This is just like some dance classes I've taken lately.

In the last chapter you learned a number of techniques for handling space problems. If you're lucky enough to be in a smaller class, you won't be bothered by them. However, dance is an art that exists in space, making it necessary for you to be conscious of where you are and what's around you from the minute you enter the studio, regardless of how small or crowded the class is.

When you make your first move into the studio you confront the moment of decision about claiming your ground. You look around to figure out where there's some space for you to work and where you think you'll be comfortable. Many dancers don't make this decision with each class they take; they simply go back to the same spot every time (or get as close to it as others will allow). Some dancers feel so strongly about working in the same place each class that they arrive at the studio extra early to be sure no one else gets to their spot before they do. If working in the same place each class is important to you, this solution is a good one.

In making the decision about where you'll work, your primary consideration should be the space that will remain between you and the next person after you take your place. Ideally there should be enough for you to extend your arms and legs fully in all directions. Take into account whether you'll be standing up or sitting down or both. Of course, you may not be able to apply this rule of thumb in very crowded classes. If that's the case, look at how others in the class have arranged themselves. Try to do the same or, as an alternative, find a place that leaves as much space as possible on all sides of you.

The space around you is your primary consideration. Equally important is finding a place that will be comfortable for you to work in. For example, in some ballet studios the barres are at two different heights: one for taller and the other for shorter people. If one of your choices of available space is at a barre that is too low for you, you'll probably be better off at the higher barre even though there may be less room there. Or suppose there's a spot near a window that's seeping cold air; again, you would probably want to look elsewhere.

As you hunt around, there'll be other things you'll want to notice. For instance, you'll sometimes see a pair of shoes or a sweater or warm-up tights placed on the floor or at the barre. This may mean that another student has already parked in the space. Without an OCCUPIED sign you may not be certain whether someone has claimed the spot or just forgotten something. When in doubt, ask whoever is standing or sitting around before you take the place.

I was warming up before a ballet class not too long ago by lying on the floor and stretching my legs out. I was about two feet away from the place I thought I had claimed on the barre. To my utter amazement, another student walked carefully around me, stepping gingerly over my head to get to the same place. I didn't say anything then, but I'd now like to give the advice that if another student looks as if he or she has a claim on a space, ask before you leap into it. It's the right thing to do.

As part of their personal development plan, some dancers may want to work directly in front of the mirror in the studio. When you're contemplating a space that puts you between another student and the mirror, and it's not clear whether being directly in the path of his or her reflection matters, ask before you plant yourself there. By the same token, if you've placed yourself in front of the mirror because you need it and someone else tries to usurp your line of vision, you're within your rights to request that he or she move.

Once you've decided on a place for yourself, be definitive about claiming your ground. Don't shuffle back and forth uncertainly. Decide where you're going to work and take charge of that spot. If you have to move to make room for someone else, you can be reasonable about it, but don't be reluctant. Establish your authority over whatever space you've decided on or moved into. Don't hug your arms across your chest, keep your knees together, or hang back. Being nonassertive because it seems more polite isn't always the best policy. Sometimes the most considerate thing you can do is to declare aggressively that you're present, alive, well, and in motion. This lets other dancers know where you stand and doesn't leave them guessing about whether they should move into the space or not.

When You Do Your Personalized Warm-up

Let's say you've now claimed a reasonably roomy and comfortable place for yourself without antagonizing anyone or creating any hazards. Along with almost every dancer who arrives at class a little early, you'll probably go into your pre-class warm-up. As you do, be conscious of where your arms and legs are going. Be sure they're not intruding on someone else. Remember also that you and the person warming up next to you may both decide to move in the same direction at the same moment. If you do so suddenly or vigorously, you won't have time to stop and avoid a collision. Try to blend the size, timing, and scope of your warm-up routine with the available space and with those around you.

Some dancers add broad, sweeping movements (like big leg swings) to their warm-up when they're more advanced. It also depends on where they've just come from (a previous class or rehearsal, for instance). If you have chosen big movement as part of your pre-class warm-up, be particularly careful about the space you have before you embark. From the opposite side of the fence, if you personally aren't doing a big-movement warm-up, you can be considerate of others who are by leaving a little extra room for them if possible.

Personal Space

Although you may not have put a label on it, you are undoubtedly aware of something that's called "personal space." In everyday existence you let strangers come only so close. It's as though there's an aura around you, and if a stranger enters that sphere, you become uncomfortable and, without even consciously knowing why, try to move away.

It may be useful when you're in class to use this concept of personal space, but to expand and understand it as "personal dance space." Personal dance space should be much larger than everyday personal space. After you've danced awhile, you'll develop a sixth sense about the size of your own personal dance space and about that needed by others in class. Needs vary from dancer to dancer, and you'll want to keep your antennae out to build an awareness about both your own needs and those of fellow students. Watch for feelings of discomfort in your dancing; as with ordinary personal space, you'll feel uneasy when your personal dance space is being intruded upon. If you have very long legs and arms, you'll likely need a large personal dance space, and the need may be very well grounded in a history of collisions with the limbs of other dancers. Try to leave a little extra room if you have long arms and legs or if you find yourself working next to a tall, lanky person.

As you grow accustomed to a class and see the same students repeatedly, you'll also learn which dancers move in a big way and which require less room. You'll even find that some dancers who are small in size move bigger than some tall dancers. Teachers are aware of these differences among dancers and may direct a "small mover" to work next to a "big mover." You can do this for yourself, too, by observing the others in your class. If you know you're a big mover, find a small mover to work beside; similarly, if you recognize one of the big movers, give a little extra room.

Your personal dance space doesn't stay in one place, of course. It moves with you as you go forward or back or from side to side, and it occupies whatever sphere you're at the center of. It's definitely harder to maintain your personal dance space and to be aware of that of others when you move off your spot. Be alert to this difference, and be prepared to handle it. For example, suppose you're about to run from one end of the studio to the other. The teacher has instructed you to go across in pairs on every four counts. Before you start out, be certain that the person who's going with you is out of your personal dance space and that the pair who were to start in front of you have actually gone, leaving enough room for you to strike out on your first step.

Dizzying turns and other difficult dance steps may send your sense of personal dance space flying right out the window. You'll simply lose control at times when you're trying to learn these feats, and find yourself intruding grossly into someone else's territory. It's often best to try out difficult movements on a smaller, less vigorous scale until you become more proficient in them, but at some point you simply have to let go and try them with no holds barred. If you find yourself encroaching dangerously on someone else's turf because you're losing your balance or the "center" of your personal dance space, stop and move back to your place before continuing. I still have scars on my hand from the fingernails of a dancer doing wild turns who refused to stop until the music did. And I'm sure someone else has the scars left by my fingernails during the times I lost touch with where I was.

Your space consciousness can't always be perfect, and if you concentrate too hard on it, the spontaneity and breadth of your dancing may leave you. Try to keep perspective on the situation. Don't let your space awareness cramp your style, but at the same time don't let your style create a space hazard.

Claiming Your Turn

Claiming your turn is another situation in which you'll want to be assertive. When it's time for you to move out—as you're going across the floor, for instance—if you hesitate or make a false start, you'll upset the pacing for the rest of the line and perhaps delay the class. Of course, starting out immediately when it's your turn isn't always easy to do. You may not be familiar with the steps and may feel nervous about how you're going to finish them once you've started. This is natural.

There are three things that can make you less reluctant to start out when you're supposed to: (1) remember that if you get mixed up, you can still keep moving along—you can run if you have to; (2) wait until the very end of the line to take your turn—that way there won't be anyone behind you to upset; (3) be sure you know what foot to start on—at least you'll be confident about your first step, and that should help you along. You can also decide not to take your turn, though if you've chosen a class that's at the right level, you probably should go ahead and give everything a try. You often learn a great deal by taking risks. Whenever you do decide to take a turn, stick with it. Clear your head as much as you can of fear and self-doubt, get ready to move, and keep moving. Don't stop in the middle of the floor or you're liable to find the person behind plowing into you.

In crowded classes, or in tap class when the teacher wants you to be able to hear your individual taps more clearly, or in ballet and modern classes to allow a rest between attempts at exercises, the teacher will divide the class into several groups that are to work one at a time in the center of the floor. Here again, it's your responsibility to claim your turn. Keep track of which group is working and when your group is next. Be ready to go to your spot promptly as the preceding group clears the floor. When you've finished your turn, move off the floor in as direct a path as you can without running into anyone.

It's often tempting to practice a step on your own at the back of the studio when the other groups are taking their turn in the center. Under crowded conditions this can be dangerous. Don't practice in the back unless it's very clear that there's plenty of space for those whose turn it is and for you too. If you're practicing in the back, also try to do the same steps as the group that's currently working. It can be very distracting if you do movement or make tapping sounds that are contrary to what the working group is doing. It may also lead to a collision, should you and someone in the back line take off in face-to-face directions at the same instant.

In general, remember that you should take the turn that's rightfully yours and not take up the space or time that rightfully belongs to the turn of another.

When it's your turn to be first in line or to be in the front line of the class, don't be timid. It's true that being first or in front puts you under pressure because you don't have anyone else to follow and are on your own to set the movement and phrasing of the steps as well as having to remember them all. You can always choose the first line for yourself, but if you haven't, and your teacher has invited you to, it's likely you're ready to accept the challenge. It's an excellent opportunity for you to try out your wings, to develop a sense of your dance independence, and to express your own personal feeling for dance phrasing. Use this opportunity to advantage by keeping your focus on the positives in the situation. The clutter of fear and self-doubt in your mind is your biggest obstacle. Once you've let it go, there's a lot more space in your head for concentrating on the movement at hand and your own growing competence.

Helping Create Unity

It's amazing to watch a group of students do the same set of movements. Each person seems to phrase it differently and to give it a slightly different impulse from everyone else. This is normal and to be expected, since there are basic differences among all of us in the way we respond to music and use our muscles. Every student can work productively in class, even with slight variations of timing, so long as these variations remain only slight. If you either race ahead of or lag behind the music too much, you can tangle in someone else's arms or legs and you may throw the timing off for the person who is directly behind you.

You should instead try to start, pace, and complete each movement combination as the teacher has instructed. If you find you can't keep up or that everything seems to go too slowly for you, perhaps you'll want to consider a class at a different level or with a different teacher. Phrasing is a very personal matter, and in some cases you and a teacher may be at extreme opposites in how you interpret rhythm and tempo. It's good for overall dance discipline to try to conform to the phrasing a teacher has marked out, but if you repeatedly find you're at odds, neither you nor the other students in the class will derive much enjoyment from it. The problem may be due to basic differences in nature between you and your teacher, and it may be difficult to overcome these.

Along similar lines you'll want to avoid consistently working on steps and exercises that are totally different from those everyone else is doing in the class. Or to stop doing a combination of steps arbitrarily and walk off the floor before it's actually over. To meet your individual needs, it will occasionally be necessary to discontinue an exercise or vary your in-class activities from the rest of the group. You may be concentrating on different technical or qualitative issues. It is certainly in order for you to do so, but if you find it necessary to do this extensively and consistently in class, you'll be expressing a lack of consideration for the teacher and the rest of the class. At the same time you'll be wasting your own resources, for if you find it necessary to deviate from the general class activities very often, it's a good sign that you're probably in the wrong place.

An atmosphere of unity is important in a dance classroom; that's *unity*, not conformity. You can still maintain your individuality while participating in class with a spirit of togetherness. Beyond the practices I've already described, you can help create a unified spirit through the quality of your attention. When your teacher is demonstrating, for instance, really watch and listen; or when he or she is making a correction on another student, again, watch and listen. Turning to the person beside you to chat during demonstrations and corrections is impolite to the teacher and the other students, and distracting and counterproductive for you as well.

There are friendlier environments in some classes than in others, but don't confuse friendliness with permission to distract and disturb. One very personable teacher I studied with created such a warm, homey atmosphere in her studio that we all mistakenly thought we were in a social club when we took class. The din of conversation between exercises was deafening. It's very nice to work in a class that has warmth and friendliness, but as tempting as side chatter may be in such a milieu, it's usually better to confine it to the times before and after class.

If your focus is on extraneous activity in class, you may miss what the teacher says and have to ask redundant questions. Or you may start an exercise only to realize you didn't watch carefully enough and can't get through it. A conscientious teacher will then take the time to repeat the demonstration so you get it right the next time. Your inattention will have delayed the class and caused you to lose your chance at the first go-round.

Arriving Late

It's a good idea to reach class in time to do some warming up beforehand, but you're not superhuman and you may occasionally arrive at the studio after class has already begun. When you do, the first thing to think about is just how late you are. If you've missed thirty minutes or more of an hour or hour-and-a-half class, it's too late to take it. You should stay to watch, though; you can learn a lot, and at least you won't have wasted your trip to the studio.

If you've missed only five or ten minutes, put your dance clothes on as quickly as possible and take your place in class quietly and unobtrusively. You might want to do a few quick exercises to warm up (for example, do a few pliés, drop over to stretch the backs of your legs, point and flex your feet), but try to join the class routine as soon as you can.

Should you catch the teacher's eye, you can express an apology for being late. Otherwise, wait until after class. Being late for dance class is like being late for any appointment and merits as much of an apology. More important, though, it merits your getting into the swing of things quickly and quietly, and creating minimum distraction from the progress of class.

Eating, Smoking, and Wearing Street Shoes in the Studio

A floor is a critical factor in all aspects of dancing. Its surface and resilience can determine how high you'll jump, how well you'll turn, and how good your knees, ankles, back, and shins will feel. Since every dance teacher in the world tries to maintain the studio floor in the best possible condition, you'll want to do a few cooperative things.

Eating in any dance studio is usually confined to the reception area. If you take food out onto the section of the floor that's used for dancing, liquid spills or globs of food that accidentally fall can create potentially hazardous stickiness or slickness. It's best to finish your snack somewhere off the floor.

Unless there's no other place for it, you'll also want to avoid eating in the dressing room. Especially in crowded studios or small dressing rooms, you'll be taking up space that might be used by other students who are changing. Think also of the danger created if someone sweeps an arm, leg, or garment in the direction of the scalding coffee you're holding. Find a place that's out of the way and that will enable you to avoid causing an inconvenience or accident.

Smoking, with the resulting ashes and butts, can also be damaging to a floor. Even when you carefully carry an ashtray with you, an unintentional flick might send ashes onto the floor, dirtying it and altering its surface. Another good reason to avoid smoking is your health. It doesn't do the other dancers in class any favors either. If you smoke, confine it to areas that are removed from the studio's dance space. Also stay out of the dressing room with a lit cigarette in your hand. Piles of clothing can easily catch fire when live ashes are dropped on them.

Street shoes and boots can be particularly harmful to a floor's surface, abrading, scraping, and dirtying it with repeated doses of grime. Your individual pair might not cause permanent injury, but the floor doesn't stand a chance against hundreds of them, over time. Take your street shoes off before you walk across the dance floor.

Personal Belongings

There are elements of considerateness, safety, and security in seeing to your personal belongings in the dressing room and in the dance studio. In the dressing room you should take a locker, hook, hanger, or space on a bench or chair, and put your clothing together neatly. In crowded or small dressing rooms, being neat and compact with your clothes is particularly important—it's the only way there'll be space for everybody to change and store their clothing.

Once you've entered the studio, store your dance bag with everyone else's. Be sure yours doesn't spread out from the pile into the area that's meant for dancing. Someone might trip over it. If you take something with you to your work spot (a towel or a sweater, for instance), put it in a place where it'll be out of the way.

Petty thievery isn't unheard of in dance studios, friendly as they may appear on the surface. Whether the job is pulled off by a stranger or a desperate fellow student, it's never a pleasant experience. Try not to leave anything you value in the dressing room. Put your money and everything else that has worth into your dance bag and take it into class with you.

The Musician

While the dance teacher is the guiding light in any class you take, the musician who accompanies class also warrants recognition. It's customary in many classes to applaud at the end as a form of thanks to the teacher. You might add a clap or two for a musician who has extended him or herself, and who has played with energy and enthusiasm. If you feel so moved, you might even tell the musician you've appreciated the effort. It's considerate and inspiring to musicians to know that their talents and work don't go unnoticed. It also pays off by creating a good class climate.

9

Next Time Around:
Taking and
Applying Corrections

A dance teacher I once knew used to be called "the disk jockey." From her comfortable armchair at the front of the studio, she'd command the class in all her corpulent splendor. After she'd told you what exercise to do and had one of the more advanced students in the class demonstrate it, she'd drop the needle onto a revolving phonograph record and stare stonily while you worked your heart out till the band on the record ended. If her gaze fell on some poor unsuspecting soul doing something wrong, she'd sarcastically badger and bark, making the student feel small and ridiculous. Then she'd sourly announce the next exercise, warn the student not to make the same mistake again, and drop the needle back onto the record. For all the teaching she did, she might as well have been a disk jockey.

This story illustrates what corrections *aren't*. For reasons I haven't come even close to guessing, a few—luckily a very few—dance teachers feel that remarks about a student's work in class must be delivered in the same sentence with demeaning comments that make the student feel like a slob. I don't consider these remarks corrections and I don't think they fit in the context of good teaching.

Now that we have that part of the issue out of the way, we can go on to the real definition: Corrections are those statements the majority of conscientious, caring teachers make, usually as encouragingly as possible, to help give students insight into their bodies and into the nature of dancing.

Types of Corrections

Generally, corrections made by capable, concerned teachers take the form of constructive, specific pieces of advice that are addressed or structured in various ways. Although there are other means of categorizing corrections, the descriptions that follow may present a useful way for you to think about them. If not, you can group them differently for yourself. Whatever makes sense to you is fine. The important thing to know is that corrections are the crux of the matter in improving your technique and increasing your understanding of dance; and that you'll make the most progress in class by attending carefully to them.

Corrections that refer to a specific part of your body (for example, "Point your foot"): Corrections addressed to one part of your body may sometimes cause you to lose track of the rest of yourself as you concentrate on that one part. Always try to integrate the correction of an individual body part with the whole. This may mean, for instance, that in applying a correction for your foot, you won't look down at it. Otherwise, you'll change the relationship of your upper body weight to your foot, and you may therefore not feel the right working sensations to go with the correction.

In fact, most corrections that single out a part of your body are meant to change your alignment so that your muscles will work correctly. For example, a correction to "straighten your knee" is really designed to line your thigh up over the lower part of your leg so that the muscles will pull up properly. When they do, this can enable you to find your balance more easily.

Since alignment is part of placement, that's the next type of correction to think about.

Corrections that refer to placement (for example, "Get your weight over your toes" or "Don't tuck your pelvis under"): Placement corrections, either for your entire body weight or for the alignment of body parts, may make you feel strange at first because they'll cause your muscles to work in unaccustomed ways. For dancing, your weight should be over your toes rather than your heels, but if you're in the habit of keeping your weight on your heels, your body may not immediately know which muscles to call upon to keep you standing. You may be shaky until you discover them, but that's to be expected. Your main task is to keep on looking for the right placement, and as your muscles work within this placement, to become familiar with the sensations.

Alignment corrections referring to a single area or part of your body often affect your entire technique. For instance, if your teacher tells you to raise your chin, the change in the relationship of your head to your spinal column may in turn change the workings of all the muscles that are attached to the spine. These include muscles that control your arms, front, and legs. Be aware that even though a correction may be addressed to one part of you, when it's about alignment it may have repercussions for many muscles and joints, even those seemingly far removed from it.

Corrections that explain the purpose of an exercise you are doing (for example, "This exercise is meant to help you feel the length of your leg, not the height of it"): Many good teachers are in the habit of regularly explaining the purpose of the various exercises you do in class. But, obviously, if they stopped to explain each one, there would be barely any time left for dancing. Generally, if you follow the directions for an exercise, you'll be achieving its purpose, even though you may not know precisely what it is. When the teacher notices, though, that the way you're doing an exercise indicates a lack of understanding about what it's designed for, he or she will include an explanation in the correction.

Explanations such as these not only improve your understanding, they also make dancing more interesting. Instead of simply going through the physical motions, you have an opportunity to think logically and productively about the exercises you do. Your "Ho-hum, another plié" can be replaced by "Aha, a plié!"

Corrections that are made in words alone (for example, "Relax you hands"): Although dance is a physical discipline, words, which belong to the intellectual sphere, are used in dance training extensively. In some advanced classes, the teacher doesn't even demonstrate the exercises; words alone are enough to communicate what's to be done. At a beginning level, however, trying to comprehend a correction that's made only in words and without demonstration can present problems, mainly because the connection between words and movement isn't very firmly established in a beginner's mind. Often intermediate or more advanced dancers may need to be shown rather than just told, as well.

If you're studying with a teacher who makes corrections mostly in words, and you sense you are not progressing as you would like to, the problem may lie in your need to see the correct way to do things and not just hear about it. You can supplement verbal corrections by watching other students. Notice when the teacher says "That's right" or "Good" to a student and try to put together the words the teacher uses in making corrections with what you see on other students' bodies. Or else consider switching to a teacher who demonstrates what's meant.

Corrections that are made in words accompanied by demonstration (for example, "This is the way to do the slide"): Any time the teacher demonstrates something, whether it's an exercise you are about to do or a correction on one you've just finished, get a good look at it. Turn around in or step away from your work space for a moment if you have to, and be sure you can see the teacher clearly. You can learn a great deal kinesthetically through your eyes.

Adjustments on your body (that is, when the teacher moves or manipulates your body or a part of it to show you how to do something correctly): Often the most direct route for making a correction is by adjusting a student's body. For example, rather than tell you to hold your elbows up, a teacher may come over to you and simply lift them.

A well-placed touch or gentle push at the right moment can save hundreds of the teacher's words and hours of your practice. There are few teachers who don't use this method of making corrections, although those who have an affinity for it use it more than others.

Students respond differently to physical manipulation. Beginners are often a little surprised at it, and some students never like to be touched. You'll find that when adjustments are made on your body by a skillful teacher, however, they're quite effective. If you dance for any length of time, you're bound to come across a teacher who uses them. Try to remain open-minded, so that if you find a teacher who's adept at them you'll be able to benefit.

Corrections that use analogy or abstraction and call upon your past experience and imagination to comprehend (for example, "It's as though a magnet is drawing your back into a curve"): Of course you use your mind all the time you're dancing—to figure steps out, to interpret what the teacher tells you, to organize your attempts at improvement. Throughout these mental activities a large part is played by your past experience and your imagination, which are some of the more powerful factors in everyone's ability to learn. Because imagination and experience provide a rich field for the growth of learning, most teachers don't confine their remarks in class to concrete, specific words. They also use analogies and abstractions.

Analogies and abstractions may be more or less meaningful to you, depending on your frame of reference. For instance, if a teacher says, "This movement is like the Trobriand Islanders' ritual rain dance," you'll probably say, "Huh?" But, in general, teachers try to present analogies and abstractions that most students can understand: "When you do these jumps, try to keep your body as quiet as a church mouse. Don't look like you've just joined the rodeo." "Think of your arms as strong branches growing from the trunk of a tree; don't let them be broken branches."[17]

A teacher who has a knack for metaphors that you can comprehend makes you feel as though you are on a marvelous journey or seeing a wonderful movie in your head as you dance. Some people, both students and teachers, just don't operate on an abstract wavelength, however. They're more accustomed to dealing with practical matters in concrete terms. If this describes you, it may take you a while to tune in to corrections that are phrased in metaphor or abstraction. Do your best to understand; it's the most you can ask of yourself. Then, if you finally catch on to them, they'll be extremely helpful. If not, though, it isn't the end of the world. There are still many other avenues through which you'll learn.

Corrections that refer to musical phrasing (for example, "Do the brushes in between the counts, not on them"): The musician is very important in a dance class. If you've ever taken a class in which the musician played poorly—uninspiredly, too fast or slow, or in an uneven tempo—you know just how important music is. Music gets into your muscles and makes them want to go—or not want to go, if it's not played well. The majority of dance teachers have decent musicians with whom they conduct class, and teachers are generally careful to coach their musicians so that the right kind of music at the right tempo is played.

When the teacher demonstrates an exercise, he or she will make a point of what you're supposed to do on which counts of the music. When it's your turn to do the exercise, however, you may not get them exactly right. You may hold a certain position a fraction too long or take a step a half-beat before you're supposed to. Sometimes these fractions and half-beats may not seem to matter. You might think to yourself, How could just a split second be that important? If your teacher makes a correction about it, you can be sure there's a reason. One is that your muscles and breathing develop in response to the phrasing you use in your dancing. For instance, if you take too long to extend your leg, you may cause your muscles to "grab" and your breath to stop. If you do this repeatedly over time, you'll develop bunchy muscles instead of long, supple ones, and your dancing may have a "tight" quality.

A second reason for paying attention to musical phrasing is that it affects your ability to do certain steps. In ballet turns, for example, if you open your arm to the side on the wrong count, or close the second arm too slowly, it will throw you off your turn. Or, in doing jumps, if the teacher tells you to be in the air on the "and" count (1 *and* 2 *and* 3, etc.), you can be sure you'll find it hard to be in the air on "1" and "2."

Any corrections your teacher makes about counts and rhythm are worth serious attention. Dancing with the proper musical phrasing can mean the difference between enjoying and fighting against the physicality of dancing.

Corrections that refer to dance quality (for example, "Make the movement softer"): Dance quality is somewhat subjective and often hard to describe in words. But it does exist, since people agree that some dancers are "fluid" or "soft," while others are "brilliant" or "strong"; or that certain movements are "percussive" while others are "flowing."

With so much focus on "steps" in dance class, you may sometimes lose touch with the very important ingredient of quality. Of course, you come to class with your own personal dance quality—a way of moving that expresses who you are as an individual and what you probably feel most comfortable doing. In addition to personal quality, however, it's important (and it can be challenging) to practice the different qualities of the various types of movement you may do in class.

If you're lucky enough to have a teacher who offers corrections on dance quality, make use of them. They may be hard to understand at first, simply because quality is difficult to describe, but when you do understand and can apply them, the scope of your dancing will broaden considerably. You'll still have your own personal movement preferences. For instance, you may have a natural leaning toward slow, extended movements. You should also be able to do allegro (fast) or percussive movements, however.

Corrections that are made to the class in general (for example, "Everyone needs to move out more in this step"): I compared notes with a few other dancers one day on our reactions to general corrections—those the teacher addresses to the whole class rather than to any one student in particular. We decided there were two extremes. At one end is the reaction "He doesn't really mean me." At the other extreme is the student who takes all corrections to heart.

The truth of the matter is that general corrections will sometimes apply to you and sometimes not. Your job is to use them when they do. Here's how:

- Don't assume that the correction doesn't apply to you until you've tried it or given it some thought.
- Try out the correction, and do it fairly. Don't go through it halfheartedly because down deep inside you believe the teacher can't mean you.
- Don't be afraid to give yourself credit if you've been objective in evaluating your performance and you feel you've put the correction to good use, or that you did the movement correctly in the first place.

Corrections that are made to individuals in the class (for example, "Joan, let your shoulders loosen up"): Just as often as you hear corrections made to the class in general, you'll hear them made to individuals. You may or may not be the individual in question. Although a correction may be addressed to someone else, however, it may still apply to you. That's why you'll want to pay attention even when the teacher is talking to a student at the other end of the studio.

Watch and listen as much as you can. This will help you build a store of valuable information you'll be able to put to good use in your own dancing. Eventually you'll be able to analyze many of your own technical problems for yourself, based on all that you've listened to and observed during classes. In a way, by watching corrections you learn to teach yourself.

Bear in mind also that your eyes can be the vehicles through which, almost unconsciously and seemingly by osmosis, your body will absorb correct placement, movement quality, and various other aspects of technique. This applies to the times when corrections are being made and to general class work as well.

When the teacher isn't addressing you directly, it may be tempting to turn to a friend and chat until the correction is finished. But turning away and tuning out at such a time is like watching every other inning of a ball game. You never know when you might miss a home run.

Watching a correction being made on another student has an additional advantage: You can be more objective about it. The teacher isn't singling you out, so you're less likely to be nervous or self-conscious. You can concentrate purely on the nature of the correction without having your attention diverted by any emotional involvement.

Corrections that are made to you personally: You can't ignore the fact that you'll have a tendency to be emotionally involved when you're receiving a personalized correction. Maybe you've just finished an exercise thinking, Wow, I really did that one well, and along comes the teacher to point out a sickled foot or to tell you that you slurred the taps in the whole last phrase. Your sense of achievement will be quashed.

When you're receiving a personalized correction, if everyone else in the class is following the advice in the last few paragraphs, you'll have a few dozen pairs of eyes scrutinizing you. You might start thinking to yourself, Is the hole in my leotard showing? Do my warm-up tights make me look fat? The extraneous thoughts running through your head can make so much noise that you won't be able to hear the correction. Obviously, you should try your best to clear your mind. Think of the correction as being addressed to your body but not to your ego. If it does drift over to your ego, take it as a compliment: The teacher thinks enough of your present dancing to put effort into helping you improve. Seeing corrections in this light may help you relax about them.

Use whatever calming or clarifying devices you can. It's natural to have feelings about being corrected, but unless they're under some kind of control, they'll clutter up your ability to comprehend and make improvement.

The Quality of Corrections

As with any skill, teaching is done better by some people than by others. And some teachers are better able than others to see a student's mistakes and to communicate how the student should work on them. Students must also be good at taking corrections, however. Basically, there are two sides of any message that concerns corrections. On the transmitting side the teacher must notice a problem, figure out what it is, think about the best way to correct it, and finally choose the best means of communicating it to the student. On the receiving end the student must attend fully and openly, translate the means of communication the teacher is using into a message that can be sent to his or her muscles, and finally apply the correction and experience the sensations of proper execution.

Most teachers are earnestly trying to meet their students at least halfway in this communication. Sometimes—whether it's because of personality factors, mood, or differences in body type between teacher and student—it just doesn't happen. It's not the teacher's fault or the student's. It just is.

You'll know when you're not responding to corrections. You won't feel you're doing well in class, and you may even begin to resent being corrected. If things just don't seem to be working out, it might be the chemistry between you and your teacher. Before you come to that conclusion, though, be sure you've taken on your half of the responsibility for the quality of corrections—that is, that you've done your best to listen to, understand, and follow them.

When Corrections Just Don't Make Sense

Even though you might ordinarily understand the corrections your teacher makes, there may be times when one just won't make sense to you. It may be a general correction made to the whole class, or it may be one that's made directly to you on your own body. For instance, James Waring used to tell me to get more "breath" into my hips. He would come over to me and poke a place in front of my hip bones that he meant. Try as I would, I couldn't understand what he was after. Breathing, to me, meant something you did with your lungs, not your hips. After I'd danced awhile longer, I figured out he must have meant that, while your hips should be held firmly, they shouldn't be "locked" into place; they shouldn't "clamp down" on the legs, even though they maintain a consistent placement in relation to them. But that took me some time to figure out.

If you've tried out one of your teacher's corrections but you can't seem to put it into operation, your first step should probably be to ask for a second explanation. This may make it clear. If it doesn't, the reason may simply be that your muscles aren't ready to connect up to what you understand in your head. You may be able to see quite clearly, for instance, that your right foot belongs behind your left knee in a particular step, but your muscles just won't coordinate your legs that way.

Or it may be that you haven't yet grasped the concept upon which the correction depends. For example, in ballet you eventually become familiar with the concept of "line"—the form your body makes in space. In order to apply a correction in which you are told to "lengthen the line of your arabesque," you need to know what the concept of line means. In an arabesque it would apply not only to the leg that's extended behind you but also to the relationship of your hip to your leg, the height of your chest, and the positions of your head and arms. Like line, there are many other concepts in dance (dynamics, projection, focus, space, suspension, rebound, etc.) that may take you a while to understand. And the corrections that are based on them may not make much sense to you until you've spent time with them.

Don't despair if you run across a correction every now and then that doesn't make sense. Instead, store it away for potential use at some future time when it may become clear. I can attest that I've repeatedly had the experience of sudden illumination about a correction (So that's what he meant!) days and sometimes weeks after it was originally made to me.

Multiple Corrections

Another circumstance under which you may be confused about corrections is when you seem to be getting too many, too fast. First you'll hear one about your feet, then about your arms, next about your back, and finally about your head. You'll be absolutely boggled trying to remember to do all the things you're being told to. Don't worry. It's normal.

In learning a motor skill (that's any involving movement of your body) you're best off concentrating on one correction at a time. Most teachers are aware of this, but they may be so ambitious and concerned for you that they'll give you a few too many corrections in too short a time. If this happens, try setting up a storage file in your head. Take down one correction at a time to apply, leaving the rest alone while you concentrate on just that one. When you think you've worked with it enough, take down the next. Don't worry if you can't remember them all, either. If your teacher has gone to the trouble of giving you that many corrections, he or she is bound to be conscientious enough to remind you of those you might forget.

Another approach is to figure out if the corrections are related to each other and, if so, to think of them together as one. For instance, a teacher may tell you to pull up your abdomen and lengthen your lower back. If you analyze it you'll realize that your abdomen and lower back are opposite each other on the trunk of your body. Instead of seeing these as two separate corrections, you can think of the one concept of smoothing both sides of your body trunk.

Feeling Guilty or Afraid

Whatever type of correction you're dealing with, above all else you should never feel guilty about needing it. Receiving a correction doesn't mean you have committed a sin or that your head is filled with sawdust. Don't castigate yourself and don't feel like a dummy. Dancing involves some very complicated coordination that has to be built over an extended period of time. Dancers require corrections at all stages of their development, no matter how advanced they become.

If you're working in class as best you know how, then you owe it to yourself to acknowledge your efforts. You don't have to make excuses for yourself or feel guilty about not putting enough into it. Dancing is hard work, it's true, but you should always try to keep some perspective on it. Judge for yourself whether you're laboring at your dancing to the point that you've stopped enjoying it. If you allow guilt to manipulate you, you'll reach that point with no trouble at all.

Fear of making a mistake, and therefore needing a correction, can also harm your dancing. It can make you hold back in your technical development and in the blossoming of your own personal dance style. Let go and take chances when you have a mind to and your body feels ready to. Even if you need some correction afterward, you'll have had the unparalleled experience of giving it a go.

Finally, don't allow any teacher to imply personal censure in a correction. If it sounds even vaguely as though a teacher is turning a correction into a maligning remark addressed to you, refuse to hear it that way. If it becomes so obvious that you can't help noticing and feeling belittled, run from the scene. Find a teacher who shows respect for the dancer and the person you are. You won't ever fulfill your true potential as a dancer unless you work in a climate that builds your self-confidence.

To sum it up, feeling guilty, dumb, clumsy, inept, or ridiculous because you need a correction, or being afraid that you might make a mistake, does very little for your dancing. Trust yourself to do the best you can, and when you do receive a correction, accept it in a positive frame of mind with a bright eye turned to the future, when you'll do it better next time.

10

Mind Over Matter: The Psychology of Taking Class

Psychology is no news to anyone. We're all aware of the effects of our mental and emotional states on our total well-being. We've heard of "the power of positive thinking" and the success you can achieve just by believing in yourself. We've also heard of the difficulties our thoughts, attitudes, and feelings can create for us. People talk about mental blocks, anxieties, and neuroses, and it's clear that these can seriously interfere with our lives.

Some features of dance classes cause psychological snags for many students and interfere with learning. They're not found in all classes, nor are they experienced by every student, of course. But there are a number of common situations that many students find hard to handle. This chapter contains suggestions for using your head to get around them. Everything won't apply to you personally, no doubt, but you may notice a few items that sound familiar.

Naturally, there will be far more classes in which you won't confront any psychological snags and blocks. In fact, you're likely to find yourself generally eager and ready to learn and conditions for learning excellent. A few hints about how to enhance these circumstances can help you in class too, so I've included them here as well.

Authority and Responsibility

> Pushkin's influence was enormous. His experience in the classroom was unmatched, and his authority unquestionable. . . . Pushkin had this ability to guide the dancer down the right path toward being realistic about his gifts, and then to inspire him to work, and work hard, at making the most artistically of those gifts. He also taught me that no one else can assume this responsibility—an invaluable lesson. He didn't force you, he gave his wisdom freely, and you did with it what you could and would.
>
> —*Mikhail Baryshnikov* [18]

It's easy for students to abdicate responsibility for themselves in the dance-class environment. The teacher prescribes exercises, establishes standards of technique, sets goals, is active in motivating you toward them, and after a while it can begin to look like all you have to do is show up for class and let the teacher take over.

I've known some teachers who are on an authority kick. They prefer that a student put him or herself in their hands and be molded. A good teacher, however, recognizes that students need to assume responsibility for themselves and allows room for this to happen.

A dance teacher's authority over you is based in his or her experience, knowledge, and skill, and a good teacher will use all of these constructively to help equip you for dancing. You must grant your teacher authority in order to learn; but you can't be misled by a teacher's commanding approach, firm manner, or strong voice into thinking he or she pulls all the strings. It's best for your development as a dancer if you participate in class not simply by following orders or being obedient, but also by taking on responsibility for your work. In concrete terms this means that you make an active choice to use all the resources at your command—your intelligence, your instincts, and your passion— to accept the goals your teacher indicates may be possible for you and then to work toward them. It's your responsibility to decide whether and how this will happen for you and not to expect that you'll be told.

Confidence

Recognizing your teacher's authority is based in your confidence in his or her ability to teach, and your trust that you'll learn how to dance under his or her instruction. Confidence or faith in your teacher is a traditional and natural part of the dance-class environment. To work harmoniously with anyone at anything, in fact, you must have faith that the other person will hold up his or her end; you must trust that the right things will result from your united effort.

Believing that you can learn to dance by studying with a particular teacher is an important ingredient in being able to learn at all. But you must also keep track of whether continued confidence in your teacher is warranted.

By all means, put your confidence in the teacher you've selected. If you've found the right one, your faith over the weeks and months of your joint effort will pay off and things will begin to click. You'll feel really good about your dancing, corrections will make sense, and you'll find yourself eager to to class. On the other hand, if none of this is happening it's up to you to take some action and not continue blindly along. Not every teacher is a Pushkin or the right one for you. Faith in your teacher is an asset, but blind faith can work against you. Keep track of your thoughts and reactions to classes and look for alternatives when you think the time is right.

Another tremendous asset to your learning is confidence in yourself. Dancers tend to be highly self-critical, and it's often an uphill battle for us to acknowledge our accomplishments or talent. We hear constant advice to be "realistic" about our abilities, and in fact most of us tend to go to realistic extremes. This can hurt a dancer's development. Of course you have to be realistic, but it's harmful if self-criticism undermines your confidence. Try to be objective about your ability and potential and about the practicality of your dance goals. Once you've done that, it's time to build your confidence. The more conviction you have about yourself, the more assurance and consistency will show up in your dancing. When you lack confidence, it's actually harder for you to do things, even those you basically know how to do well.

You can promote your own development as a dancer through the confidence and faith you put in yourself during classes. This means taking corrections with a positive outlook and starting all the dancing you do with the expectation that it's going to work. It means not apologizing for yourself if you make mistakes, and looking for new challenges and opportunities to experiment with. It means not being afraid that you'll fail, and knowing that you have untapped resources and alternatives if things don't develop exactly as you expect. In sum, believing in yourself works for you; doubting yourself works against you.

Level of Involvement

There are many of us who dance because somewhere down deep inside we absolutely must. Choice almost doesn't exist for us, and no matter how we go about arranging our lives otherwise, we always come back to dancing. Some of us enter performing careers; others perform for a while, then teach or choreograph; and still others, while they never appear on the stage, take classes regularly and wouldn't dream of spending their free time any other way. These are the addicts among us.

Then there are people who take class because they want some form of physical exercise—some way to keep trim or to balance the mental gymnastics they go through in their daily lives. Exercise not only strengthens the body, it also can relieve mental and emotional stress, help you sleep better, and generally contributes to a fuller, more enjoyable life. Because dancing does all these things and more, people who choose it as their form of physical exercise sometimes become as addicted as performing professionals.

Students take dance classes for other reasons, too: because they like the ballet and want to know more about what they're looking at; because their best friend is taking classes; because they've tried ten different exercise schools and have finally found in dance a physical activity that doesn't bore them silly.

To a large extent, the psychological factors at work for you in dance class depend on the intensity of your involvement. Performing professionals do tend to be more deeply involved, if only because they spend more time at it than nonperformers. But any dance student, regardless of professional goals, can become quite serious about classes. This is all fine. Dedication to an art feeds your energy and your motivation and can be a critical ingredient in your development—so long as it doesn't lead to a takeover by negative influences like anxiety and worry.

Students who are deeply involved in dance can put themselves into a frantic state, fretting about their technique, rushing around to try this teacher or that one, becoming seriously depressed when they don't meet a goal they've set for themselves. Being involved with dancing but keeping enough distance so that you remain calm and clear is no simple balancing act. Anxiety can be rampant almost before you know it's knocked at your door, and asking it to leave can be like trying to remove gum from your shoes.

If the level of your involvement with dance has grown so deep that it looks like a matter of life or death, it's certain to stand in the way of your learning ability. It will interfere with your concentration, your appetite, your coordination, and a myriad of things that go into making classes productive for you. If you have set your sights on dancing with a company and it just doesn't seem to be working out, you can improve your state of mind if you realize your alternatives aren't exhausted. You can head in another direction. If your technique has a few flaws in it that you can't seem to conquer, the best thing you can do for yourself is to understand that you aren't stymied. You can work on perfecting the things you do well. (There's a ballet superstar—whom I won't name—who can do turns only to the left, but those left-sided turns are a knockout.)

Grim determination and stubborn tenacity really aren't good for your dancing. Yes, you'll want to work hard and to develop your potential to its fullest. But for that to happen, you must leave some slack in the reins. There has to be play in them to give your dancing the latitude it needs to grow. A good sense of humor is especially useful to dancers. You can be deeply involved in and committed to dancing, but try to allow yourself the freedom to laugh at yourself and at the sometimes-ridiculous situations dance leads you to.

A lighter involvement with dance is precisely the right approach for many students—adult beginners, for instance, who take one or two classes each week and who may miss a few every now and then. The only time a light involvement can be troublesome is when you expect too much.

You can learn to do a great deal of dancing by taking class fairly regularly twice a week, but it will never turn you into a performing professional. Don't become frustrated because you think you should be doing better than you are. If you've set aside only so much of your life for dancing, and have filled the rest with your career and other activities you enjoy, keep your expectations in proportion. Don't let frustration ruin the pleasure you take in classes. You can still do your best and try your hardest in the classes you take, and you'll actually learn more and do better if you quit worrying about what you can't do and simply enjoy what you can.

Feedback

"That's right." "No, that's wrong." "That's better." "Now you're dancing!"

Feedback—one form of which is the information a teacher gives you about your performance in class, telling you whether it's good, not so good, or in the middle—is essential to your learning. In addition to providing a reading on how close you're coming to the standards set by your teacher, feedback may be expanded to include a correction or explanation of what you should do differently. As you already know, corrections are indispensable in learning to dance. Feedback, even without an explanation, is equally important; if you don't receive enough of it, you can head in the wrong direction and have a hard time getting back on track.

SOURCES OF FEEDBACK

In dance class your teacher is one of your primary sources of feedback. Dancing is not like sports, where you receive feedback through visible end-results—a ball that goes through the basket, a home run, a puck in the goal, a tennis ball your opponent can't hit back. These are all things you can see, and the coach doesn't have to tell you that you've done them. In dance, by contrast, you can't always see what you're doing, and consequently you need someone out there who can.

A second type of feedback you receive in class is from your reflection in the mirror. You can actually see, in this case, the lines and shape of your body, and can compare them with the goals you're striving to meet. When your focus must turn from the mirror, though—as you move across the floor, or when your head drops over or faces away—this form of feedback is no longer available to you.

The third type of feedback you use in dancing is internal. It's in the form of sensations that come from your muscles. To be useful for dancing, internal feedback has to be tied to the right goals. In other words, you have to know what a step or movement is *supposed* to feel (or look) like before you can pick out the internal sensations that belong with it. And this takes you back to your teacher.

Your teacher will tell you a great deal about how dancing should look and feel, and will be instrumental in helping you hook up to the internal sensations that are so important as a source of feedback. After you've danced awhile, the associations between your internal cues and your outward movements will come more quickly and will need less coaxing from your teacher. In fact, you'll often know from your internal feedback whether you've done something correctly even before your teacher has given you external feedback about it.

The problem is that you can't train on the basis of internal feedback alone. Sometimes it plays tricks on you—like fading in and out of focus or deciding to go on an unannounced holiday. These are the times when you have to depend more on external feedback, and particularly feedback from your teacher (rather than from the mirror). Internal feedback also has a habit of getting out of whack if you don't take class regularly. Fortunately, when you return to class your teacher's eye will still be its old reliable self, and by giving you external feedback he or she will put you back in touch with the right inner sensations.

Since feedback from a teacher is so important, you'll want to study with someone who gives enough of it—a teacher who corrects you, who tells you when you've applied corrections well, and who gives you frequent information on how you're doing. The more personalized the feedback is—that is, the more it's addressed specifically to you—the better, though of course you benefit from generalized feedback, too.

POSITIVE AND NEGATIVE FEEDBACK

Most teachers are aware that feedback comes in both positive and negative packages. With a good teacher, negative feedback ("No, that isn't right") is always accompanied by a correction or explanation ("What you should do instead is . . ."). A good teacher also usually gives positive feedback ("That's better," "Now you've got it," "Good") in plentiful doses.

You need negative feedback to help you correct your mistakes, and you need positive feedback both to tell you that you're on your way to correcting your mistakes and to keep your spirits up. In both its general form ("Good, everybody!") and its personalized form ("Good, John!"), positive feedback makes things better and more enjoyable.

Negative feedback at times gets a leg up on positive feedback, perhaps because the teacher notices a great many problems that need correcting, or because he or she loses track of the balance between the two. In addition, teachers are human beings. They don't feel as "up" on some days as they do on others, and it will show in the amount of positive feedback they give during class.

When positive feedback falls below a certain minimum level, its lack can cause your dancing to deteriorate considerably. There aren't too many teachers who forget about positive feedback, but a few do exist. To give you an example of one extreme, I took class twice a week for a full semester with a man who either said nothing to students or criticized them mercilessly. If I hadn't needed the course credit, I would have dropped out. The experience was so demoralizing that I didn't go near dance classes for a month after the course ended. Fortunately for other students, the teacher was replaced soon afterward with a more conscientious one.

There are a number of teachers who don't make much use of positive feedback but compensate for it in other ways. For instance, they have an excellent "eye" and are able to give you corrections that help your dancing enormously. Or they'll phrase their criticisms so neutrally and with such obvious concern for your dancing that you won't miss the positive feedback at all. Of course, if you feel you do, it may be time to start looking around for alternatives.

Competition

In the American tradition of free enterprise and athleticism, competition can be found all around us. Many of us do well in competitive situations. They seem to drive us to bigger and better achievement and to make success even sweeter. Then there are those of us who compete well in some circumstances but prefer not to contend against rivals when it comes to other matters. And finally there are many who basically just don't like competing at all. It makes them tense and prevents their full enjoyment of any activity.

Dance classes can be very competitive, with students constantly vying for the teacher's attention and continually conscious of how they're doing as compared with the rest of the class. If someone else does a kick up beyond shoulder height, they'll try to do one up beyond their ear. If another student does three turns, they'll try to do four. Teachers may encourage this kind of contest among their students, or it may just arise because most of them are naturally competitive.

Feeling as though you're in a race or trying to win a game when you're in class may or may not suit you. It leaves some students absolutely turbulent and it's a hindrance to their performance in class.

If you seem to react poorly to competition, there are a few things you can try: (1) When you watch other students in class, focus on what you can learn from them, not on comparing yourself to them. (2) If you think you'd like to be able to do what they're doing, analyze how they're achieving the results. (3) By the same token, don't look at students who aren't doing as well as you are in order to feel superior. Watch them to see whether you can figure out what they should do to improve their dancing.

In addition to trying to learn from rather than compete with other students, you can occupy yourself with what you're feeling about the movement you're doing. Experience all the internal sensations you're capable of and, in relation to the outward environment, cultivate the perception of your body moving through space.

The music or accompaniment is another element with which your mind can be more constructively occupied. Listen to it closely. You'll find that sharpening your attention to the sounds will help your dancing at the same time as it releases you from the pressures of competing.

It may happen that none of these approaches will work for you and you'll begin to bite your nails and dread going to class. The question to ask then is whether you're in the right kind of environment for your particular dance development. It's a question to talk about with friends, family, your teacher, and anyone else you think might help. A poor response to a competitive class doesn't mean you should stop dancing; it just means you might have to look elsewhere to find your niche.

Measuring How You're Doing

It's natural to be concerned about the level of your technique. Part of the enjoyment of dancing is the experience of knowing you've gained enough control over your body to express yourself through movement, and when you've set a goal for yourself, it's reasonable to want to know how close you're coming to achieving it.

As any scientist will tell you, though, once you try to measure something, you run the risk of altering the thing itself. Your attempts may move it, reshape it, make it smaller, or have an even more fundamental effect like changing its chemical structure. You can minimize these risks if you use good measuring techniques, and the ones that follow are meant to accomplish this for your dancing.

THE RIGHT KIND OF COMPARISON

As you've just read in the last section, many dancers can't effectively or productively measure their progress by competing with or comparing themselves to other students. I believe that the best kind of comparison to make—the kind that will help you to make the most progress—is one in which you evaluate the difference between what your dance capabilities were before and what they are now. Are you stronger than you were last year? Do you seem to grasp steps more quickly? Another dancer may be stronger or quicker, but that's not important. Don't waste your time comparing yourself to students who are equipped or gifted in different ways from you. Instead, when you want to analyze how you're doing, think about the things you can do now that you weren't able to do before.

TESTING, TESTING

Most people don't plan on having a complete medical checkup every day, or every week or month, for that matter. It would take too much time and money and wouldn't be that helpful in getting through life. In the end checkups that occur too often are just a waste.

Dancers sometimes involve themselves in the equivalent of a daily checkup. They fret over how many pirouettes they've done, how high they've jumped, or how fast they've tapped every day. It's natural for that to happen, because you do in a way test out your body each time you go to class.

I don't know about you, but whenever someone says the word "test" to me I leave the room as quickly as possible. It reminds me of those Sunday nights before the Monday-morning spelling quiz, or those last hot days in June when I sat, cramped and sticking to the seat of my student desk, trying to remember the date when the Great Wall of China was built.

Trying to judge how well you're dancing too often is like making yourself take unnecessary tests. It's unrealistic to expect that you'll improve with each class; you may during some phases of your development, but during others it will feel as if you're going at a snail's pace, if not backward. You'll develop greater consistency of technique as you become more advanced, but even the most talented dancers have days, performances, rehearsals, and classes that are better than others. Measuring your achievements too often can be as much of a waste of time and money as having a daily medical examination.

It's best to learn how to wait, especially when you're just beginning—to allow yourself time to absorb and evolve. In one of her most-quoted remarks, Martha Graham tells us it takes ten years to make a dancer. Certainly you'll feel you're dancing before then, but mastery of your body takes time, and if you rivet your attention in every class on putting yourself to the test, you'll miss the point and the sensations of dancing. Have faith in your ability to learn, and spend your time giving yourself encouragement instead of seeing whether you've scored 85 or 90 percent on the last exercise. You'll be the first one to know when your dancing is improving (or perhaps your teacher will be the first, but you'll be a close second). So just keep up the good work and don't worry about passing any examinations.

SETTING GOALS TO MEASURE YOURSELF AGAINST

To measure your progress realistically and coherently, you may want to set some specific qualitative and quantitative goals that you feel are important and that are reasonably within your grasp. Be clear and precise about them, and don't put the entire universe of dance technique into them. For instance, suppose you want to increase the stretch in the backs of your legs. One measure of the amount of stretch you have there is whether you can touch your fingers to your toes. Depending on your body structure, you may eventually be able to stand with your knees perfectly straight and put your palms on the floor. Figure out where you are now—perhaps you can touch your ankles—and set the next goal for yourself: touching your toes. Once you've reached that goal, go on to the next: putting your palms on the floor. If your body allows you only to reach your shins, though, don't make your initial goal putting your palms down. You'll wind up forcing and frustrating yourself unnecessarily.

Qualitatively, you might want to set goals for the ease and fluidity of your stretch: Hunching up your shoulders and getting red in the face is one way to touch your toes. But you'll probably want to set the goal of making it appear effortless and even enjoyable.

Remember not to check yourself against anyone else as you're trying to reach the goal you've established for yourself. Also don't check on yourself every day. Give yourself weeks, perhaps months, depending on how far you start from your goal. You may do your stretching exercises daily and casually observe how close you're coming. But don't create a pressure situation for yourself every time you attempt it.

Realize, too, that your body will vary. Your legs may tighten on some days and, after you thought you'd reached your goal, you'll find yourself unable to perform as you did on the preceding day. Don't worry. If you've done it once, you'll be able to do it again.

There are many stunning and complicated feats you can set as your dance objectives. There are also many simple yet beautiful accomplishments you may wish to attempt. Find those that appeal to your sense of aesthetics and that seem within your body's grasp. It is not necessary to perform multiple pirouettes or split your legs or wrap your foot around your neck to dance. Pick and choose among the alternatives, and don't assume you must do all that you've seen—or any that you've seen, for that matter. Keep looking until you find what's right for you, then set your goals—clearly and realistically—and work toward them calmly and collectedly.

SLUMPS

Dancers commonly experience periods in their development when they don't seem to make any progress. A dancer may go from the beginner to the advanced level in two years, for instance, and then spend months without any improvement whatsoever. This may happen for several reasons and at any stage of development. It may be due to the fact that muscles require time to learn coordination. You can't do anything to speed them up; they simply need a certain amount of repeated exposure to what it is you require of them. The repeated exposure also must be spaced; you can attempt to acquire the coordination of a motor skill by practicing it a hundred times in one hour, but the results will be far better if you do it a hundred times over the period of a week. Of course, it also depends on the skill to be learned and on the person. Some skills are generally easier than others, and some people seem to be more natural at acquiring them, needing fewer practice runs in total and less spacing. But the "naturals" get stuck too. It just seems to be a fact of life in learning motor skills.

If you find yourself not making any progress for a while, don't despair. That's the least constructive action you can take. Becoming worried and frantic won't help either. Simply recognize that you've run into an obstacle, but one that's not insurmountable. Then develop a plan to help yourself around it. Your plan may be as uncomplicated as waiting it out—giving your muscles the amount of practice and the time they need to connect up to the skills you're after. Or you may try a change of teacher, school, class, or type of dance. Keep calm as you follow your plan, and don't keep checking on yourself to see if you're out of the slump. Stay attuned to your bodily sensations, invite the encouragement of friends, and continue to maintain respect for yourself as a dancer and as a person.

PHYSICAL LIMITATIONS AND OTHER FLAWS

While a slump is something you know you'll come out of, you may find it harder to deal with a physical limitation or a flaw in your technique that doesn't seem to respond to your efforts.

Your natural physical endowment includes such basic elements as the lengths of ligaments. Take the one that crosses the front of your hip joint, for instance. This ligament, known as the Y ligament, holds the front of your thigh bone to the front of your pelvis so that when you try to lift your leg to the back it prevents your going beyond a certain point. It's designed to prevent your thigh bone from slipping out of the socket where it belongs.

If you have a long Y ligament, you'll probably be able to lift your leg higher behind you than a dancer with a short one. If your Y ligament is short, you can work on stretching it to increase your range of movement; but no matter how hard you try, the ligament will stretch only a certain amount. There's no need to feel defeat or disappointment about a short Y ligament. It really has very little implication for the totality of your dancing. While you may be short on a ligament, you may be long on the other qualities that make an exciting, expressive dancer. Being depressed about a physical limitation can only hold you back. Accepting it for what it is will liberate you to go on to other things.

There are many types of physical limitations that you can eliminate. For instance, when I first started dancing I had extremely weak ankles. Even as a child, when I didn't dance, I remember spraining one ankle or the other a couple of times a year. Weak ankles are a definite limitation for any dancer, but you don't have to live with them. I did special ankle- and foot-strengthening exercises daily for a solid year to overcome the problem, and I've suffered only one sprained ankle in my entire dance career since that time.

Flaws in your technique can sometimes be overcome head on; sometimes they need an indirect approach. If you're unable to do pirouettes on one side, for instance, you might follow the example of the ballet superstar I mentioned earlier and learn to turn very well on the other side. Or, as another example, suppose you've studied ballet all your life and now want to try a modern technique. You start modern classes only to discover that all your years of ballet training prevent you from using your body as freely as the modern technique demands. You can't seem to drop your weight into the ground enough, and your muscles won't respond in the right ways. Your modern technique has so many flaws in it, you don't know where to begin. Do you have to dismiss the whole idea of modern dance? Probably not. What you're likely to find is that the flaws that seem so numerous are all based in one or two problems of dynamics. Once your body solves these, the individual flaws will disappear rapidly.

In general, physical limitations and technical flaws can't be met effectively with a worried attitude. Nor do they always respond to direct confrontation. A flexible, problem-solving approach, in which you keep yourself free to try various alternatives, is a better way to tackle them.

Two-Way Communication

In accordance with tradition and protocol in dance training, and also because it's more efficient, you'll find that the teacher does just about all the talking in class. As a student you'll have minimal opportunity to say anything while class is in progress, and although many teachers invite questions ("Is that clear?"

"Do you understand the step?"), generally you're expected to be silent. The assumption is that you're there to dance, not to engage in verbal dialogue.

Most students will tell you they prefer it that way. If they stopped too often to ask questions or speak at length, their muscles would never warm up and no dancing would get done. However, you personally may find yourself wanting to ask questions or to have things explained. You might be the type of person who approaches classes with a great deal of intellectual curiosity. The traditional conduct of the class may not seem to allow ample time or opportunity for questions and explanations, though. Should you just grin and bear it? Wait until you grow used to it? Figure that two-way communication just doesn't belong in dancing?

To the contrary. Two-way verbal communication is very important in learning to dance. Although it can't be very expansive during class time, when you must keep moving, there often can be a perfect opportunity for it after class. Students tend to forget their questions by the time class is over, or feel it's not worth bothering with them. But your questions are an asset in your learning. Psychologists say that a person learns better when allowed to seek information actively rather than when sitting back as a passive receiver. Letting questions form actively in your mind and then pursuing the answers is an excellent learning technique.

It's true that there's significant physical content to master in dance, and we may therefore mistakenly assume that the only way to learn dancing is to do it. While physical practice is an absolute must, you can't neglect the contributions of your head. If you're the kind of dance student who seems to have a great many questions, seek answers. If you haven't already found one, look for a teacher who seems to enjoy explaining things and who takes the time to describe and enlarge upon steps and movements. Such a teacher will answer many of your questions before they're completely formulated in your head, and those that do take shape will be dealt with fully and clearly—both during class and afterward. Teachers can be very cooperative and useful if you give them the chance by talking about what's on your mind. Not every last one will be, it's true; like other people, they have their ups and downs, and some are just more open to dialogue than others. Your best bet is to try. If it works out, that's great; if you run into a stone wall, then you might have some serious reckoning to do. You may be tempted to avoid the issues and suppress your questions, feelings, and concerns about dancing, but that never eliminates them. They often go deeper and grow out of proportion when you don't let some realistic two-way talk shine on them.

Attention Span

Children generally have a much shorter span of attention than adults. Attention span varies also with the day and your state of mind. In general, though, any time you want to increase your ability to concentrate, the best approach is to do it without pressuring yourself.

Don't arrive at class thinking you're going to pay fierce attention the entire time, and then get angry with yourself when you discover your mind has wandered. Your muscles won't work if you lock them into position, and neither will your mind. You must let it relax and breathe, just as you do your body.

You should come to class expecting to pay attention in segments you can comfortably handle. You might, for example, think of each exercise as being made up of several segments: the demonstration by the teacher, a quick run-through in your head, and then your performance of it. You should try to free your mind of anything extraneous as you work, and look for only those things that apply to each segment. After you've finished, you can let your mind shift to a different level of attention.

Actually, the dance-class structure is a natural for helping you concentrate, because there are intrinsically two basic levels of attention you pay. One level is for performing the exercises, when your primary focus is on the connection between your mind and your body. The other level is present between exercises, when you're intent on listening to the teacher's instructions and using your powers of comprehension on a more purely intellectual level. You can build the habit of an easy flow from one level to the other, and this in itself will create the mental breathing that you'll operate on most effectively.

You must also expect that your mind may still wander off during class, even though you let it breathe. You probably know the experience: The teacher has just finished demonstrating a step and when the music starts you realize you neither saw nor heard anything about it. Your mind was miles away.

The worst thing you can do when your mind wanders is to become upset. This will only distract you more. Rather, simply acknowledge the fact that your head took a brief sojourn, and go on to the next event. If it's another exercise, try the segment routine once again.

You can also encourage your attention to function better in class if you give your mind a chance to warm up. You arrive at class in time to ready your muscles beforehand. Why not do the same for your head? Start your mental warm-up while you're working on your body. Concentrate on your sensations. Notice whether your hips feel tight or loose, how the floor feels to your feet, whether there's tension in the back of your neck or your shoulders. See how far your breath can reach into your torso. Notice whether the backs of your legs feel stretchy. If you've come to class with a load of life's problems on your mind, try to replace them with an awareness of these sensations. Let more and more problems slip away as greater space in your head is filled with contacting your physical self.

You might not need a mental warm-up for every class. There'll be times when you arrive already alert to your body or with a completely clear and quiet mind or bursting with enthusiasm to begin class. If you're taking tap, you may notice that, regardless of the mental state you arrive in, something magical happens with the first exercise, and everything else that's on your mind drops away. For many classes, though, you'll find a mental warm-up as necessary as a physical one. The reason, of course, is that it's more natural to treat yourself as a unit and not separate the activities of your physical self from those of your mental self. Try it and see if it doesn't make a difference in your dancing.

Motivation and Discipline

Nothing will spark your learning like your desire. Wanting to learn to dance can be the biggest factor in enabling you to find the means to do so. Generally speaking, you probably won't encounter a more-motivated group of people than those in a dance class. The students who are there have all made an active choice in the matter, and are present because they very much want to be.

Your level of motivation will probably be quite consistently high in dance class, provided you don't pick up interference from any of the troublemakers mentioned in this chapter. To further maintain your motivation at a good, healthy level for class, it should also be at a good, healthy level in the rest of your life. You must be motivated to feed yourself properly, to rest enough, to arrange your schedule so that you take classes often enough, and to keep some emotional balance in your life. You can think of your general motivation as the support system for the specific motivation you need in class.

People often talk about discipline when it comes to dancing. But "discipline" has a negative ring to it; it sounds like punishment or something that's imposed on you. I like to think of motivation right along with discipline, because motivation comes from inside you and causes you to do the right things for your dancing because you want to. You may find it useful to think of the partnership of motivation and discipline in this way, too.

11

In Your Mind's Eye:
Mental Practice
and Mental Images

In 1967 an article was published that described the results of a series of experiments in mental practice as applied to sports.[19] "Mental practice" is defined as performing a physical activity in your head without using your body. In other words, instead of actually shooting baskets or jumping hurdles, you just imagine you are. This kind of "imaginary practice" is supposed to improve your performance.

How is this possible? No one is exactly sure. One theory is that mental practice has something to do with motivation—the more motivated you are, the more you'll want to improve, and using mental practice just tends to reflect or heighten your motivational state. Another theory is that when you imagine a movement, you actually send "action currents" or slight nervous impulses to the muscles that are supposed to be used during the movement. Although these impulses remain beneath the conscious level and don't actually move any muscles, they are rehearsed subconsciously by your nervous system, so that when you next try the skill, the right impulses are there to be called upon. Since muscle action is totally dependent on nervous impulse, once the right impulses are there, the right muscles will also be.

Whatever the explanation, the results aren't surprising, because your mind and body are a unit. What you do with one is bound to affect the other. It's best, of course, if you do both imaginary and physical practice. This makes sense, both because you achieve the most success when you integrate your mental and physical experiences and because you can't build the required strength and stretch in your muscles unless you actually use them. But even by itself, mental practice can be effective. During a period when I was off my feet with an injury, I practiced pirouettes in my head for several weeks without doing any physical exercise whatever. When I returned to class, my pirouettes were consistently good even though the rest of my technique was shaky.

Image Quality

You need a "good image" to make mental rehearsal work for you. A good image is one that accurately represents how the body should look or work when doing a movement. You can use an image or picture of your body in action, or you may use a picture of an object or a mechanical device that looks or works as your body should. So long as it correctly represents your anatomical structure or the mechanical dynamics of the movement to be performed, it will be useful. Let's take an example.

Suppose you want to improve how you move up to a passé position. As you raise your knee, it's important to keep both your hips on the same level, and not to let the one on the side of the rising leg get higher than the one on the side of the standing leg. If you use an anatomical image, you might visualize your

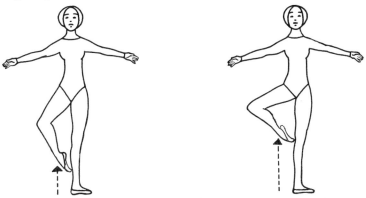

hip bones staying along the same horizontal line as you raise your knee. This would be a good image because your hip bones

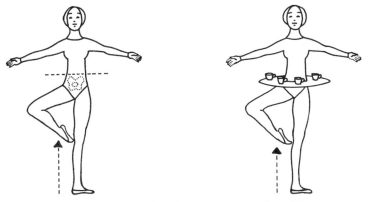

are clearly where you need to focus your attention. If you use an object image, you might see in your mind's eye a tray with teacups on it that is sitting at your hip line and that you don't want to tip on its side. This is a good image because it will help your muscles to work equally on both sides of your body, just as your two arms would work equally to balance the tray.

You need to be familiar with the physical skill you want to perform in order to use mental images effectively. In fact, imaginary practice by itself probably won't help you much until you've had some physical involvement with the skill you want to work on. You can't hold a really good image in your mind until there's some physical experience to hang it on. Beginners may therefore be able to use images successfully only when they are in class, combining them with physical practice. For all levels of dancers, however, images can be extremely powerful, and the better their quality, the greater their effectiveness.

Acquiring and Maintaining Good Images

One of the functions of your dance teacher is to provide images that you can apply to your dancing. Some teachers are better at suggesting them than others, and there are a few you'll find who will give you vivid pictures that will work like magic to enable you to improve your dancing.

You must also develop images for yourself, however. Because no two bodies are exactly alike, you need to create images that take account of the differences in structure and function of your own body. You'll achieve better results than if you use your teacher's images only as exactly suggested. You might begin by following an image suggested by your teacher, but you will sometimes find it more effective if you then modify it to suit your specific needs. When you reach a higher level of understanding, you may originate images for yourself on the basis of what you know about the idiosyncrasies of your body or on the basis of an insight that no teacher has yet presented to you.

Images tend to wear out after a while, too, and you need to renew them in order to keep your nervous impulses from going stale. Good teachers understand this instinctively, and change or refocus images for you all the time. But you may also have to do it for yourself when your particular body no longer responds to an image you or your teacher suggest to it.

Specific Images to Use

You can think of mental images as being of two different types: (1) those that deal with the coordination of specific skills (turning, leaping, jumping, and so on); and (2) those that depict how to use a part or area of your body.

The images you might use to practice the coordination of a specific skill will depend on how your teacher presents it, on your stage of learning, and on the particular points you need to think about to account for the uniqueness of your body. Images for a coordinated skill may therefore vary quite widely. To give you an example, I'll describe the image series I've used for a ballet pirouette. Keep in mind, however, that this may not be the right series for you or the one that your teacher recommends.

PIROUETTE IMAGE SERIES

The first image I see for a pirouette is the preparation. I'm firmly in a fourth-position plié with arms prepared:

Next I see my forearm open and a strong horizontal line take shape across my back. Simultaneously, I see energy pressing down through my heels and my plié strengthening.

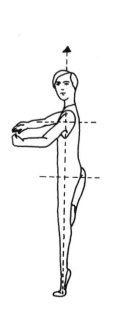

When my arm closes and I rise onto half-toe for the pirouette, I immediately see a straight line ascending through my body, and I add a second horizontal line through my hips. I also see my head remain front as my body turns away.

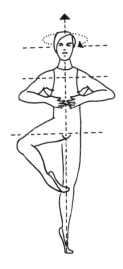

Finally, my head flips around to finish the turn with my ears remaining on the same horizontal level and the straight line continuing its energy upward through my body.

If you've ever tried a ballet pirouette from fourth position, this sequence may make some sense to you. There are many other image series you can use. The one I chose worked for me because I had particular problems remembering to press my heels into the floor during the preparation, to keep my back square, and to leave my head behind long enough before turning it.

Besides images for coordinated skills that will depend on your teacher, your stage of learning, and your particular body, there are other images that are useful for some basics of human movement and muscle action. Those described here are based primarily on ballet technique,[20] but they represent the kind of good body mechanics that apply universally to many different types of movement. You may find them useful not only in ballet, but also in tap, modern, and jazz dancing—even in ordinary walking.

IMAGE FOR THE LOWER BACK AND CENTER TORSO

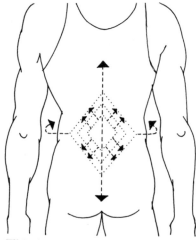

See a diamond shape at the small of your back. Energy emanates from its center. Two of its points are directed straight up and straight down; the others are directed to wrap around to the front of your waist.

This image will help to increase the space in your lower back and will prevent the vertebrae from squeezing together in that area. It will also help you to achieve firm support in the central area of your torso.

IMAGE FOR THE UPPER BACK

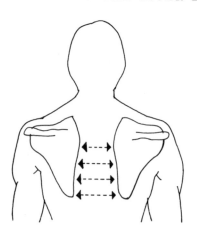

See a space between your shoulder blades with energy spreading out to either side. This will keep your upper back strong and will prevent you from "pinching" your shoulder blades.

IMAGE FOR YOUR NECK

Visualize your neck as a channel that must remain open for messages between your head and body. See it as clear of obstruction and constriction, and as a straight, easy path for the messages to flow through.

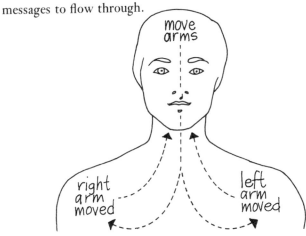

This image should prevent you from straining your neck and help you to keep your head centered over your spine.

IMAGE TO RELAX YOUR SHOULDERS

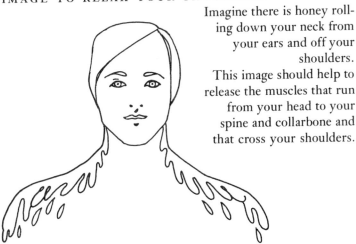

Imagine there is honey rolling down your neck from your ears and off your shoulders.

This image should help to release the muscles that run from your head to your spine and collarbone and that cross your shoulders.

IMAGE FOR TURNOUT

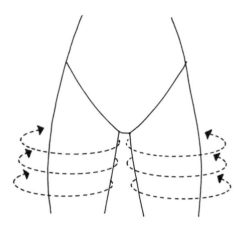

Visualize energy radiating from the tops and insides of your legs, around to the backs of them. This image should encourage you to work your turnout from your hips rather than from your knees or feet.

IMAGE FOR PLIÉ

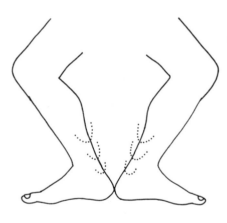

See the muscles in your calves oozing down toward your feet. This will help your muscles to relax; it will deepen your plié and make it more elastic.

IMAGE FOR YOUR FEET

See your toes spreading out on the floor with energy directed outward from each. Use this image whether you are barefoot or wearing shoes.

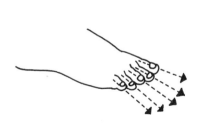

This image will prevent you from rolling in on your arches and will keep energy extending out through your toes, which you need for your leg muscles to work properly.

IMAGES WHEN YOU STAND ON HALF-TOE

See an arrow descending between your first and second toes. This image will help you to keep the weight of your body properly placed over your toes and will prevent your rolling out in the ankles.

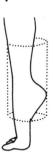

See a hollow cylinder encasing your ankle and supporting it equally on all sides. This image will help keep your ankles from wobbling.

These are just a few of the hundreds of images that you may find will work for you. Your teacher will suggest many more, and as your technique develops you will begin to create some for yourself.

Devising Your Own Images

For any coordinated skill, the best way to develop a mental picture of it is to watch someone carefully—your teacher or another student in the class—who performs the skill correctly. Look at it closely and try to pin down the important details: the dynamics, the placement of body parts, the rhythmic impulses, the starting and finishing positions. The image should be like a full-color motion picture that you can project on your mental screen and watch as an audience would in a movie theater.

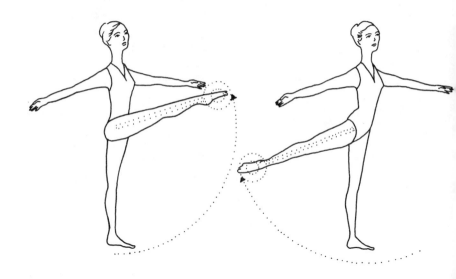

You can also draw on mechanical devices you're familiar with to create images. For instance, in visualizing the action of a leg swing, you might see it as a pendulum.

If you are developing an image that pertains to an area or part of your body rather than to coordination for a skill, one good approach to use is to learn about the operation and structure of the muscles and joints involved.* For instance, the image of the diamond at the small of your back is based on the fact that muscles run up and down your spine and wrap your body in that area from back to front.

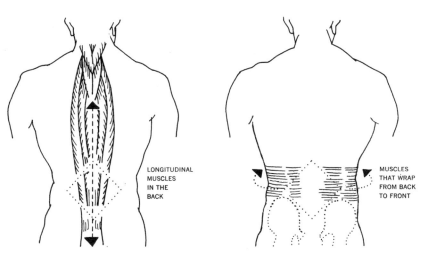

LONGITUDINAL
MUSCLES
IN THE
BACK

MUSCLES
THAT WRAP
FROM BACK
TO FRONT

For your own personal development, you'll want to use images that meet your special needs. Be on the alert for them. Try all the images your teacher suggests during classes, even when they don't seem important. Sometimes an image your teacher mentions casually just once is exactly what you'll need to help you over a technical problem.

*See Chapter 13 for suggestions on how you can learn some anatomy.

How and When to Use Mental Images

Most often you'll use mental images while you're in class. Although it's possible to use them in separate mental-practice sessions—I'll describe how you do this shortly—most students put images into operation during the time they spend in class, because that's when the teacher suggests them and there's the opportunity to apply them.

USING MENTAL IMAGES DURING CLASSES

A technique for using mental rehearsal during class that you may find effective is to flash an image across your mental screen a split second before you're about to do a movement. With an image of total movement coordination for a skill, you should do the mental rehearsal only in the split second before you do the movement, and then let it go. Don't try to hold on to the image while you're actually doing the physical performance. It will just get in the way.

When you're working with an image of a specific body part or area, you can rehearse the image in your mind both before and while you're doing the physical performance. For instance, if you're using an image for relaxing your shoulders, you can visualize it before the movement. Then you can also continue to use it while you're doing a tap routine you've already learned, say, or while you're running or leaping. So long as you don't have to think about the coordination, you can use your mind to focus on an image for a body part or area.

USING MENTAL IMAGES IN SEPARATE
PRACTICE SESSIONS

When you do mental practice in a separate session, it's usually best to put your body in a neutral position. The constructive rest position,[21] in which you lie on the floor, is a good one. (It must be the floor that you lie on; a bed or couch won't give you the proper support.)

In this position the arms are crossed comfortably on the chest and the knees are raised and together. If your arms don't fall comfortably on your chest, you can drop the elbows down and let your hands rest on your rib cage. If your legs seem to fall out to the sides, you can tie them together loosely just above the knee with a scarf. Or try putting your feet in a pigeon-toed position and leaning one knee against the other.

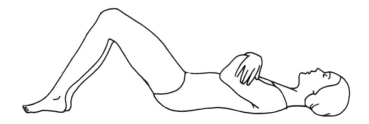

Adjust yourself on the floor until you feel you are settled nicely and easily and you sense that your body is lined up from your head to your toes. Now you're ready to close your eyes and practice an image. The image may be one that involves movement, or it may be one in which you work on a particular area of your body. Be certain you have a good image—one that correctly represents the skill you want to practice or the body area you want to improve. Make the image as clear and as vivid as possible.

See yourself going through the motions of any movement that's involved, but don't tighten or tense any muscles. The success of mental practice depends on your not using any muscles consciously. You are addressing only your nervous system at this point, encouraging it to learn the right impulses to send to the right muscles. Your nervous system learns this coordination on a subconscious level, and the minute you start confusing it with conscious muscle contraction, you prevent it from finding the proper nerve-to-muscle pathways.

To sum up, when you're involved in a mental practice session that's separate from physical practice:

- Make sure you have a very clear, precise, and vivid image of the skill you want to practice or the area of your body you want to address.
- Incorporate images that point out the particular difficulty you may be having with the skill or area.
- Put your body in a neutral state such as the constructive rest position.
- Don't voluntarily contract any of your muscles while you're doing the mental practice.

Generally, a mental-practice session should last no more than ten minutes. During this time you can work on just one image or on several. Use each one repeatedly, being careful to keep it in sharp focus. When you find yourself growing tired of working on one image, go on to another. At the end of the session roll onto your side and lie still for about thirty seconds. When you rise, don't make the transition too abrupt.

Problems with Mental Images

When I first experienced the results of using mental images, I was astonished. I thought that at last I had found the secret of learning to dance. Unfortunately, while mental images are extremely powerful aids to your dancing, they aren't the total answer. You must still mix mental images with physical practice, and no one has yet been able to figure out the best ratio of one to the other. Another problem is in constructing good images. An image that your teacher suggests may work for a fellow student, for instance, but not for you. And before you can create effective images for yourself, you may need to learn a great deal about body structure and function and movement dynamics.

Even more problematical is that physical practice sometimes

works against the mental practice that you do. You simply can't run through a mental rehearsal, no matter how brief, or use a mental image for every last move you make in dance class. You must fall back on established "motor programs" or "muscle memory," or else you'd never move. When you walk, for example, you don't flash a mental picture of yourself walking before you take off. A subconscious part of your brain has "programmed" all the nervous impulses and muscles you need to put one foot ahead of the other. You decide to proceed from one place to another, and off you go. Similarly, after you've practiced various dance movements, you don't have to think about their coordination. The movements are programmed into your nervous system and your muscles remember how to work in the movement. You simply decide to move and the motor program takes over.

Difficulties arise when your motor program isn't exactly right. It may send impulses to the wrong muscles or at the wrong time, and although you'll be headed in the right direction, the coordination won't be precisely the one you need. Even though you'll try to reprogram yourself through mental practice, the old motor responses will be so established that you'll automatically revert to them. Of course, the less embedded the wrong motor program is in your repertory of skills, the easier it is to replace with a new, correct program, so this may not be as discouraging as it seems. But still, your use of images may not be as successful as you would have hoped.

As I've already mentioned, mental images do tend to wear out, so you must always be on the hunt for new, correct images to replace those that no longer work. This takes dedication, experimentation, and time.

Despite the shortcomings, however, using mental images infinitely helps your dancing. You'll want to find and apply as many good ones as you can, because they will serve the very important function of integrating your head and your body and enabling you to dance as the total mental and physical entity that you are.

12

But You Should Have a Degree: Studying Dance at Colleges and Universities

As listed in the 1976 *Dance Magazine Directory of College and University Dance*, 170 colleges and universities offer degree programs or courses of study in dance.[22] In 1960 there were only 67. Obviously, there is considerable and growing interest in pursuing the academic route to dancing.

In your own case you may choose a college dance program because it's the only solution when you and your parents decide you can dance but you should also have a degree. Or you may seek a degree in dance because the college setting provides a spectrum of dance and dance-related studies you can't get anywhere else. Or you may start out as a math or English major and just fall into it.

There are pros and cons for going after a degree in dance, on either the undergraduate or graduate level. There are also a few myths. Before discussing the pros and cons, I'd like to dispel the myths and state some biases.

Myth #1: If you want to dance professionally, you won't make it going to college. True for ballet dancers, maybe (though there are a number of colleges that offer a ballet major and are affiliated with a local performing company). The myth is totally unfounded for modern dance, however. There are just too many college graduates who have danced or are currently dancing professionally. (See the rosters of the Murray Louis and Alwin Nikolais companies; the Martha Graham company; the Merce Cunningham company; the Viola Farber company; and on and on. Also note Patti D'Beck, who is in the cast of *A Chorus Line* and at the same time working toward a degree at New York University.)

Myth #2: You won't find good technique training at college. This supports Myth #1, and is equally as absurd. You can sometimes find better instruction at college than you could ever hope to find elsewhere, even in New York City. You can choose a college dance teacher as successfully on the basis of reputation and background as you can a studio teacher. And there are plenty of good technique teachers to be found at colleges and universities.

A likely advantage you'll have at college that you might not have in a New York City studio is more personalized attention. You'll tend to form close ties with your teachers and grow to know them well. In addition, dance has a special status in academia that breeds a feeling of "We're all in this together." At highly competitive studios such as you'll come across in New

York, the prospects for togetherness are pretty bleak, and your technical development may suffer because of it.

Myth #3: There are very few jobs for people with degrees in dance. This is a borderline issue. I think things are changing, but I can't dispel the myth entirely. It's true, however, that you stand a better chance of landing any teaching jobs that exist if you have a degree. Many students find jobs at the schools where they practice-teach, an opportunity you'd never have under any other circumstances.

The other benefit is that by taking a variety of courses, as you do in college, and not studying technique alone, as you might at a studio, you increase the number of job prospects open to you. Dance-related and other courses might lead to a career as a dance therapist, writer, critic, choreographer, press agent, photographer, stage designer, stage technician, or costumer, for example.

I and the people I interviewed in preparing this chapter* have a number of opinions about studying dance in college, and most of them are good. For example, we think:

*My thanks to: Laura Brittain (B.A., Theater, UCLA, 1968; M.A., Dance, UCLA, 1971; formerly a member of the Gus Solomons Dance Company; currently directing and choreographing for the Washington Square Repertory Dance Company; Assistant Professor, NYU Department of Dance and Dance Education); Leon Felder (B.A., Dance, Bennington College, 1975; currently teaching and performing with his own company in New York); Dana Johnson (B.A., Dance, Denison University, 1975; M.A., Dance, NYU, 1977; currently dancing in New York); Leslie Seaman (B.A., English, Colby College, 1970; M.A., Dance, NYU, 1976; currently choreographing for the Washington Square Repertory Dance Company and teaching dance at Brookdale Community College, N.J.).

And special thanks to Professor Judith Schwartz of New York University's Department of Dance and Dance Education for her careful review of this chapter and her excellent suggestions.

- You'll receive a tremendous amount of encouragement at college of a kind you'd never find anywhere else. (During the interviews I heard remarks such as: "A lot of people showed faith in me." "There was a great deal of personal caring." "I felt close to the people in the department; they were very supportive.")

- Opportunities for experimentation are all around you. You'll try yourself out in any number of roles and activities. (Interviewees said: "We had dance happenings all the time." "I performed with Steve Paxton in New York when I was still a freshman.")

- The philosophy underlying most college and university dance programs is that students should have opportunities to find what suits them best. Thus, several techniques and styles of dance are usually offered and you are encouraged to experiment with them all. The environment will support your thinking about the various dance choices open to you and will address you as a total being and not just a physical entity. You'll learn to dance, but you'll also learn to think and choose.

- Along similar lines, you study a host of dance-related subjects and as a result your understanding and ability as a dancer and as a person grow more than they would if you took only technique classes. (Interviewees said: "It's wonderful to be a technician, but there are other important things to know about dancing." "Technique just isn't enough for everyone." "If you're serious about life, you have to do more than study technique.")

With myths and biases now clearly stated, we can look at the pros and cons. A college program isn't the right answer for everyone, and certainly you can learn about life and dance in ways other than by going to college. But if you're thinking about it for yourself (or your son or daughter), here are some things to weigh.

Commitment

One big advantage to having an academic degree in dance as your objective is that the subject gets your full attention. You make an unequivocal choice to dedicate your time and energies to it. Often dance studies have to play second fiddle, but when you pursue a degree, you, whoever pays your tuition, and everyone else in the program have concurred that dance is worthy of a serious investment of time and attention.

Being in a degree program means that you set aside a piece of your life to devote to dance studies. You don't have to juggle your activities or sandwich dance in, and you don't fall into the pattern of saying, Maybe next year . . . Once you're in the program, next year has finally arrived, and with it a vast array of experiences and opportunities in your chosen field.

Resources and Facilities

Colleges and universities comprise a collection of people, books, classrooms, equipment, and facilities that are meant to encourage learning. Nowhere else do you have such a concentrated gathering of resources directed to the study of the arts and sciences.

TEACHING STAFF

Dance teaching staffs vary just as do the staffs of any other discipline. Some staffs are excellent; others are more average. A number have a faculty star or two in the shape of a well-known choreographer or performer. Currently there are more qualified teaching candidates to choose from simply because there are more people dancing, and more of them are seeking educational careers in dance. Another rich source of teachers can be found in the guest artists that colleges are inviting more and more often to conduct workshops and special courses. Well-known dancers and choreographers accept these assignments because they are some of the best job opportunities around. A guest artist's engagement can range from a day or a weekend to a quarter, semester, or full-year appointment.

On the negative side, dance faculties can often be quite small, having one department head and only two or three other teachers for the entire dance curriculum. This won't leave you much choice when it comes to decide with whom you'll take a course. A small faculty also may mean that individual members are overextended and called upon to teach many more courses than they can prepare for adequately.

STUDENTS

You might not think of it at first, but the other major human resources at any academic institution are your fellow students. Exchanging ideas and experiences with the people you meet in classes is an excellent learning activity. You benefit from their thoughts and at the same time have the chance to speak your own mind. You seek opinions and express your own and in the process develop a point of view and reasons for it. Discussion also stimulates you to think and often to do things that would never have occurred to you unless you began talking in the first place. Undoubtedly you'll find some souls more kindred than others, but because you'll have exposure to quite a few, you're bound to locate a number who'll speak your language.

LIBRARIES AND AUDIOVISUAL FACILITIES

A collection of books and films on dance can usually be found in the library of the dance department itself or in the central library of the school. Magazines and other periodicals about dance are normally available as well.

At New York University's Bobst Library there is even a librarian who specializes in dance. A dance librarian can be extraordinarily helpful when you're tracking down information for a research project or when you need other material that isn't immediately obvious on the shelves or in the catalog.

Have you ever seen yourself dance? (Other than in a mirror, I mean.) Many colleges have videotape cameras, decks, and monitors that either are the property of the dance department or can be borrowed from another department. Watching yourself on video is a revealing, enlightening experience that can spur your development. If the equipment is available, you can usually find a student volunteer to run it. In some instances part of your coursework will include making a videotape of your dancing, and all the arrangements for it will be made by the instructor.

PRACTICE, REHEARSAL, AND PERFORMING SPACE

Spaces to rehearse and choreograph in are also usually provided for students so that they can work on their technique and create dances. Before I began my master's-degree program, all the dances I choreographed had a very strange floor pattern because I had to allow for the furniture in my living room. Once space becomes available, your dances can become quite liberated.

For performances you don't always need (or want) a formal theater. In fact, many dance experiments of the past decade have taken place in other locations. The lawn, the art gallery, the library steps, a plaza, or a corridor can all be the scene of a campus dance performance. Students and faculty will be your ready-made and handy audience, and the buildings and grounds office will usually be cooperative if you give them enough advance notice of the impending event.

OTHER DEPARTMENTS

Essentially the resources of the entire university are at your disposal. Your interests in other fields (aesthetics, philosophy, music, psychology, whatever) can be satisfied by the many courses offered at the school. If you don't want to take them for credit, it's often possible to audit, which at some schools means you won't pay tuition and won't be required to do the papers and other assignments for the course.

Along similar lines, interdepartmental cooperation for other purposes may also become a resource for you. For instance, the theater department may decide to produce a musical that requires a choreographer. They'll call up the dance department, and you may have the chance to do your first show. If you need extra dancers to fill in some numbers, you can give your fellow students a chance to perform, too.

Or an administrative group (for instance, the registrar's office) may decide they need a physical-fitness program and want dance classes for the employees. If you're interested, you could design and teach the sessions and chalk up some adult-education experience to your credit.

Performing Opportunities

Performing opportunities are plentiful in almost all college and university dance programs. Since dance is a performing art, most schools try to integrate performing with as many courses and academic activities as possible. You'll take courses in choreography, for example, where you'll perform in your own dances and other students'. Each fall and/or spring there's likely to be a concert in which you'll appear in a dance you've created, perhaps, or in that of another student, a faculty member, or a visiting choreographer. Inevitably, someone will have an idea for a workshop performance or improvisation that you'll want to participate in. If you take a course in dance production or if you belong to the dance club, you're bound to find performing opportunities there too.

Ties with the community will also present chances to perform. Public schools, hospitals, libraries, social clubs, prisons, and other community groups often are delighted to engage student performers as part of their special-events programs, and many schools make a point of keeping in touch with these organizations to let them know that students are interested in performing for them.

Naturally, all your performing opportunities won't be as grand as you might like them to be. You may not always appear in works you love, for instance. Not everyone is a Martha Graham or a George Balanchine, and any budding choreographer must experiment with a number of false starts. You may have to put up with old equipment or a student stage crew who are brand-new on the job and a little unsure of their cues. But all of these conditions may exist even when you dance professionally. So long as you experience dancing on the stage, no matter what the circumstances, it will feed your developing ability as a performer.

Developing Dance Technique

I've already addressed the myth that good technique training can't be had in college. The type of training you receive in college depends on the same variables as it would at any place of study: the quality of the teaching, the adequacy of the facilities, your own talents and abilities, your approach to classes, and the time and effort that go into it.

If you are careful to look into the background and reputation of the staff and to find out about guest teachers who have been at the college in the past, you shouldn't have too much trouble selecting a college where you'll be able to develop a solid technique. (Later in this chapter I'll talk more about evaluating dance programs.)

There are a few things that may bog down your technical development, though. One is the workload from other courses. For Dance History 101 you'll have a paper, for example, and eighty pages of reading to do each week. You may have to take a course in movement analysis or Labanotation and spend hours observing movement and figuring out how to write it down. You might, as a result, miss your technique classes for days on end to complete your other coursework. Or you may spend your first semester at school fulfilling prerequisites and have time for only a few technique classes each week.

Another potential problem is that instruction in ballet technique at some colleges may not be as solid as it is in modern dance technique. Historically speaking, modern dance wedged its foot in the academic door more firmly than ballet managed to. Many colleges and universities are catching up, though, and quite a few now have outstandingly good ballet classes among their departmental offerings. If you want to study ballet technique, you'll have to be sure you select a place that has competent ballet instruction.

Some dance techniques may also be totally lacking at college. Jazz, for instance, appears here and there among colleges, but tap can be hard to find. That means that if you aspire to a job in musical comedy, you may have to pick up jazz and tap elsewhere. With a good ballet or modern foundation, though, you shouldn't have any problem taking them on.

Course Requirements, Grades, Tuition, and Other Bureaucratic Issues

COURSE REQUIREMENTS

There are arguments on both sides of the course-requirements question. One side says that required courses are a drag and asks why students shouldn't be able to decide for themselves what courses are right for them. Who's paying for it, anyway? The other side says you might miss something you really need if you're allowed to choose everything on your own. A required course might even introduce you to a whole new field you never thought you'd like.

Required or not, courses that most dance departments offer do round out your understanding of and appreciation for the art. They can help your technical development too. Music, theater craft, Labanotation, movement analysis, anatomy, kinesiology, dance history, dance criticism, and dance composition build your grasp of the hows and whys of dance. You'll find that the courses all interrelate after a while, so that your studies in dance history, for example, will be food for thought in composition class, and your work in anatomy and kinesiology will help you in your technique classes.

In spite of the fact that course requirements exist, there is often great leeway within the courses themselves. The objectives set for them, whether required or elective, can in many cases be met in ways that are individual to each student. For instance, in dance history you may choose to research a period and write a paper, or you may instead conclude your research with a dance you've choreographed in the style of the period.

Life experience may also count toward your degree in some colleges. If you've taught or performed or choreographed, and you have substantiating evidence of your work, you may be able to waive some requirements.

GRADES

Earlier I mentioned that you're better off if you don't give yourself grades in technique class. Most college courses do tag a grade on, however, and knowing that the instructor will be giving you anything from an A to an F can make you tense and hinder your enjoyment and learning. I tried not to let it bother me; I actually threw out my grade envelope without opening it when it came in the mail after my first semester. But other students inevitably raised the topic, and soon I was wondering and worrying about grades as much as anyone else.

Do grades really matter? After all, there's always a subjective element involved in the teacher's evaluation of your work or performance. Your own evaluation may be as valid. What's the difference between an A− and a B+ anyway, and how much

importance does it have for whether you can dance or not?
Grades are an unruly issue, and in response to the sentiments
of some student bodies, many colleges have modified their grad-
ing practices. A few are on a pass-fail system and don't give
grades at all. Some require that, instead of grades, instructors
give written descriptions of each student's work in a course,
with suggestions for areas of improvement and special commen-
dation for outstanding accomplishment. At still other colleges,
each student sits down with each of his or her teachers to
discuss the evaluation entries that will go on the academic
record, and nothing is put in writing until the teacher and student both agree.

TUITION
Tuition costs go up every year at colleges and universities,
and there are relatively few scholarships, assistantships, and
fellowships offered for dance students. There's never any harm
in looking for financial aid to put yourself through college, although you'll have to do a lot of hunting to find it for a dance
degree. Some state universities can be attended free, but at the
high end there are private colleges that cost $4,500 a year.
Men, take notice: Money may be more readily available for
you than it is for female students. This is done to encourage
more males to enter the field of dance. Yes, it is sex discrimi-
nation, though any man who is given a financial award must
have at least a moderate share of talent.
If meeting tuition and other living expenses is going to be a
problem for you, you can think about a part-time job, either at
school or in the community. Investigate these opportunities before you enroll so that you'll know you have an alternative to
dropping out because you run out of money when you're only
halfway through. The college or university will provide information on financial aid and work availability.
Another alternative is to attend a college or university you can
afford, even though you know it doesn't have exactly the pro-

gram you want. You can transfer after a year or two if your financial status improves. Or else find a school that allows you to attend as a part-time or "special" student, taking just a few credits each semester. The important thing is to begin your studies once you've decided that's the direction to go in.

BUREAUCRACY

The threat of rampant bureaucracy is present any time you have an organization. In an academic institution you'll find such examples as "Students must register for courses no later than September 1 or pay a $5 late fee," "The deadline for submission of the master's thesis is April 15," "Each dance major must attend at least three meetings of the Graduate Dance Club each semester."

Making and enforcing rules and regulations are the legacy of all those in the administration who must keep the institution viable. You'll sometimes see the reasons for red tape, and you might agree it's necessary. At other times it will make you furious because it stands directly in the way of your graduating or doing what you think is best for you, not the institution. You eventually learn how to maneuver past bureaucratic hassles, though, and I believe that progress is being made toward minimizing them in many dance programs.

Making a Trial Run

Many colleges and universities offer summer programs that give you a taste of the academic dance life. Connecticut College in New London has the most famous one. It may be well worth your while to invest in a summer to see how you like it before you commit yourself to a full-fledged academic program.

You can obtain information on summer college dance programs from each May issue of *Dance Magazine* and also from their *Annual*. Keep your eye on the March and April issues, too, for ads placed by the various colleges and universities that have summer programs.[23]

Non-degree College Dance Programs

Let's say your final discussion with your parents about what you'll do with your life after high school ends at one in the morning. You've been back and forth over the issues and have finally reached a compromise: You'll go to a college where you can major in something useful (that is, a field that has more potential for a paying job) and minor or take some courses in dance.

This is not an unreasonable solution to the dance-versus-career debate. Getting a degree in another field doesn't exclude the possibility that you may dance professionally. (To give you just a few of the many current examples, James Teeters of the Alwin Nikolais Company has a degree in mathematics from Dartmouth College; Moses Pendleton of Pilobolus Dance Theatre has a degree in English literature, also from Dartmouth; and Alison Becker Chase of Pilobolus has a degree in history and philosophy from Washington University.)

To protect your interests in dance when you undertake another major, you should peruse the college's dance offerings carefully. Use the information on evaluating college dance programs in the next section of this chapter.

If you can't find a college or university that adequately fits your needs both in your major field of concentration and in dance, try to locate yourself near a city where you'll be able to take studio classes. Enroll in the college or university as a part-time student if at all possible so that you'll have a reasonable amount of time and energy for dancing.

Finding and Evaluating College and University Dance Programs

The *Dance Magazine Directory of College and University Dance* is an excellent guide to consult. You can find it in a public or school library, or you may want to order it from *Dance Magazine*.[24]

Before you start hunting for a school, you might want to set some basic limits such as location and cost. You'll be able to find information on location, tuition costs, and the availability of financial aid in the *Dance Magazine Directory*. In thinking about costs, remember that you don't have to eliminate a school because it at first looks too expensive; there may be various types of financial aid available.

Your next concern should be whether the school offers the kind of degree program you're after. If you already have an undergraduate degree, you'll seek a place that offers advanced degrees. Do you want a performing specialization? Look for a B.A. or B.F.A. on the undergraduate level, and on the graduate level an M.A. or M.F.A. with a concentration in performing arts. Do you intend to teach? Look for a B.A., B.S., M.Ed., or M.S. with a concentration in dance education. Not sure whether you want to perform, teach, choreograph, write, become a dance therapist, or pursue some other related area? Look for a place that offers a diversified program in which degrees with various specializations are offered.

Do the best you can to narrow your choices, then obtain a catalogue for each place you think is a possibility. Libraries often stock them, or else you can write to the college for one. With catalogue in hand, look for the dance program under such headings as "Dance Department," "Theater Department," "Performing Arts," or "Physical Education," and see if you can ferret out answers to these questions:

- *What is the ratio of faculty to number of courses taught?* A good rule of thumb is that there should be at least one faculty member for every three or four courses offered. You may have to hunt through the catalogue to find all the full professors, associate professors, assistant professors, instructors, part-time teachers, and teaching assistants and fellows who belong to the dance department.
- *Are both modern and ballet technique classes taught?* A few colleges make ballet a specialty. With most, though, modern dance is the principal offering. While your preference may be for modern, you may also want to take ballet classes as foundation for your overall dance technique.
- *Is there a variety of courses to choose from?* This question is especially important if you're not absolutely certain about your interests and want to experiment with several approaches to the study of dance (for example, history, teaching methods, dance therapy, ethnic dance, jazz, tap, dance composition, movement analysis). Also be sure that the academic side of the curriculum looks as strong as the technique side.
- *How many years will it take you to complete the program?* See what the prerequisites are and whether you fulfill any of them. Determine whether your previous experience or academic credentials count toward the degree. Estimate roughly how long it will take you to complete the program you're thinking about, and see if this fits your needs. For example, at New York University's School of the Arts, a master's degree in dance with a concentration in performing requires three years for most students to complete. At New York University's School of Education, a master's degree in dance with a concentration in education or dance therapy usually requires two years.

- *What is the tone of the department as it comes across in the catalogue?* Does it sound innovative or stodgy, forbidding or friendly? Is there much talk about rules and regulations and little about creativity? Do the course descriptions sound exciting?
- *If faculty biographies appear in the catalogue, what are their backgrounds?* Are there any who have been with professional performing companies? If you're stage bent, you'll definitely want a teacher who's had performing experience. Most catalogues list at least the degrees each faculty member has. Look the list over. Are the degrees in dance or in dance education? If your interest lies in teaching, try to find at least one faculty member who has a degree in education. Not sure where you'll end up? Look for a good mix of performers and educators among the staff.

The catalogue can tell you only a limited amount, of course. You still have more to find out before you can narrow your choices further and make your decision. Word-of-mouth is an exceptionally effective way to obtain information on a dance program. Ask among friends and dancers you know if they can tell you anything about the schools you're considering. Ask if there are any others they've heard of or can recommend. You might also try writing to the head of the dance program at each place you're interested in for the name of a recent graduate living in your area whom you could call. Gather as much data as you can about the reputation of the school. Reputations always have some basis in fact.

If you can, you should also try to pin down other specifics. You may be able to do so by reading the catalogue, talking to alumni, or by writing the school directly and asking:

- *Did they have any guest teachers or artists-in-residence last year?* Who were they? What were they there to do?

How long were they there? Does the department plan to continue having guest teachers in the future? guest choreographers? Choreographers and professionals who are invited to campus to perform, choreograph for students, and teach will liven the atmosphere as well as impart skills and information. They are a wonderful shot in the arm for both faculty and students. In addition, bringing in guest teachers or artists-in-residence is a sign that the department has enough financial backing to run a diversified program. See if there's anyone you've heard of among the guest artists they've invited, or consult a dance encyclopedia to find out more about them.

- *How many scholarships (fellowships, assistantships) are available for dance students?* How much can be offered? How do you qualify? Scholarship availability and amount may be another indication of how committed the school is to the dance program, though a lack of scholarships doesn't necessarily mean a lack of commitment.

- *Do professional dance companies appear regularly on campus or in a nearby community?* Dance students should see as much dance as they can, but professional performances may not be readily accessible in out-of-the-way places. A school may have many things to recommend it. If it also offers performances by professional companies, either on campus or nearby, you'll be that much better off.

- *How many student performances are usually given during a semester?* Where are they held? Do students have opportunities to perform before community groups?

- *Does the school have an affiliation with any professional or semiprofessional performing company?* How do you get into it?

- *What kinds of practice teaching opportunities are there?* Can you teach children? adults? fellow students?

- *How many dance majors are enrolled in the department or program?* How many students (majors, minors, and those from other departments) generally attend technique classes? You want enough people around to make classes dynamic, but you don't want to get lost in the crowd. One of the advantages of being in a place that's not overcrowded is that you receive personalized attention and encouragement. A technique class maximum should be about twenty to twenty-five, a minimum about ten.
- *What are the dance-class facilities?* Are the studios designed for dance or are they old basketball courts? You can dance on a basketball court, but a studio is usually better.
- *What are the library and audiovisual facilities like?* Do you think they'll be adequate for your interests and needs?
- *What are the theater facilities like?* If you're a performance-oriented student, look for a good theater with good lighting and sound equipment. Find out if there's a lighting director or if the theater department assists in dance productions.

As you narrow your choices further still, if it's at all feasible you should visit the one or two colleges you think are the likeliest candidates. When you're there, talk to as many people as you can. Students already in the program can be especially helpful. Find out what at least three or four of them have to say so that you hear different points of view. Ask for permission to watch technique classes and to sit in on any courses that interest you. Evaluate the technique classes using the guidelines from Chapter 1 of this book.

While You're Attending

When you're installed in school, take advantage of all possible opportunities that conform to your interests and needs. For instance, if you think your ultimate goal is performing, perform whenever you can. Go to auditions if they're held and tell other students you'd like to appear in the dances they choreograph. Want to teach eventually? Take on any relevant assignments you think you can handle. Try teaching all ages and all types of people until you've identified which you like best. Is choreography up your alley? Don't be shy about performing in your own works and asking fellow students to perform in them. Solicit their comments and criticisms. You may never again have such a receptive, constructive climate as you do at school.

In general, go to see as many performances as you can, both on and off campus. Take master classes with visiting artists when they're offered. See any dance films that the school owns or rents. Don't miss any event that you think has the slightest connection with your interests. Go to faculty-student teas or whatever social gatherings give you the chance to chat with teachers and your fellow students.

Leave time for your course work, naturally, and follow the same practices any other student would to meet course obligations.

Give yourself at least a full school year to decide whether it's working out. If you think not, don't be afraid to transfer. Contrary to what people may tell you, if you have sound reasons to do so, transferring doesn't hurt you. Because a school isn't right for you doesn't necessarily mean it's a bad place. All it means is that it didn't suit you, that you couldn't get the exposure to experiences you thought you needed, or that there was a poor fit between your interests and the program offerings. Talk things over with someone who'll be able to grasp your situation—a teacher you know and like who has a background similar to yours, for example. Or a student you know who's transferred from another school and seems to have interests like yours. In some cases, you may want to go directly to the head of the department, air your grievances, and ask for his or her advice. After you've thought and talked about it, if you decide it's right to switch to another school, do it.

Concerning transfers, if you've started out in another major only to find that dance is your true passion, you may want to change departments if not schools. It may be well worth the loss of a few credits. There are countless numbers of students who have stumbled onto dance as first-year majors in other fields, and who have been nothing short of ecstatic with the change to dance.

When You Have Your Sheepskin

Students who enter college with a clear idea of their career objectives are rare. Many of us even graduate without being certain about what we really want to do. Taking the first job that comes along or putting ourselves into a situation we hope will lead to a good job are two approaches we commonly use. With good fortune, we end up doing what we love. Here are some hints to bring you closer to that blissful state of affairs:

If professional performing is your bag, hie yourself to the places where the action is.[25] If you make the most obvious choice—New York City—you'll have many good studios to go to, and you'll be in the best place to make contacts for job openings. The competition is heavy, but if you have conviction and confidence, you're willing to work hard, and you can dance, there's very little that will hold you back. You may not join one of the larger, better-known companies right away, but you can get good experience working in smaller ones.

Above all, broadcast your interest in performing. Many of us are shy and demure, well-mannered and quiet, hoping someone will notice us one day if we hang around long enough. Be clear and loud. State your interest to any choreographer whose work you like. Ask if you can study with him or her and mention that you'd like to join the company eventually. Find out if there's an upcoming audition. Also keep in mind that many choreographers choose people for their companies from among their students, so don't depend exclusively on auditions.

Graduates who want to try a teaching career must first decide on the level at which they'd like to teach. Prospective elementary and high-school teachers, TAKE NOTE: Complete those education courses you need for state certification. These vary from state to state, so be sure you take the ones that are right for the place you think you'll teach. Most states don't certify you in dance, only in physical education. Take whatever courses you need as part of your degree program so you won't have to waste any time after you graduate. Prospective college and university teachers, TAKE NOTE: You're likely to need a master's degree to teach at the college level. Plan accordingly.

For teacher job openings at the elementary and high-school levels, consult your adviser and contact the board of education of the locale in which you'd like to teach. College and university openings are often advertised by flyers sent to your dance department. Also consult the "Personnel Vacancy Listings" in each issue of the American Dance Guild *Newsletter*. [26]

As I mentioned earlier, students who have not majored (or even minored) in dance need not eliminate a dance or dance-related career. So long as you've had some background, you may be able to go on in the field. You can pursue a performing career or, if you have a bachelor's degree, go after an advanced degree in dance. Make use of your best realistic tendencies, but don't give up your dreams too easily.

Should you come to the conclusion that dance isn't right for you after all, there's no reason to despair. At least you'll have a degree, and whether it's in dance or anything else, that piece of paper is a minimum requirement for many jobs you may want.

13

Beyond the Physical: Reading, Research, and Other Activities to Help Your Dancing

Dancers are action-oriented people, liking especially the experience of digging in physically to things. We may at times be so committed to the physical realm that we find ourselves very impatient with pure rational analysis, introspection, or contemplation. This may be particularly true when we approach the field of dance itself, in which we're so accustomed to involving ourselves first and foremost on a physical level.

Of course, there's nothing like experiencing movement to give you physical as well as intellectual insight, and that's what makes it so fine. But for those of you whose usual operating style is to analyze a bit and to be curious in an intellectual way, doing some reading and research in association with your physical plunge may be just the thing that will open up new possibilities and dance opportunities for you.

Obviously, the fact that you're reading this book is a sign that you're somewhat thoughtful about your dancing. And you may therefore be open to many of the suggestions that will be made here as well as those I've already mentioned. In this chapter the reading and research recommendations are presented in cafeteria fashion. Just as you don't eat all the items on the cafeteria counter, so you won't necessarily follow all these suggestions. Choose those that suit your taste and your current involvement with dance, and that will mean the most to you.

Dance History

Although history to many people means wars, dates, and a generally allergic reaction, to dancers it can mean more positive things. Through a number of books covering various periods of dance history, you can become acquainted with the development of dance forms and with the social and cultural influences on them. If you're just beginning to consider which type of dance to study, knowing something about the people and events behind the forms in existence today may help you decide which you'll undertake. It's akin to reading about a country you're going to tour.

If you're already committed to a particular type of dance, reading dance history can deepen your appreciation of it. Learning how a type of movement evolved can give you insight into why classes are structured the way they are or why you dance in a particular way. For instance, if you're a modern dancer, you might be interested in learning that the first modern dancers took off their shoes so that they could be closer to nature and to the natural movement they wished to explore.

Professionals preparing to perform roles often will read about the works they're to appear in, and if it's available may go into the history of dancers who have previously performed the roles. Such historical information is frequently found in the form of magazine and newspaper articles and reviews published at the time the works were performed. Thus, for a complete historical picture, it's necessary at times to go not only to books but to periodicals as well.

Biographies can be especially enlightening, since they're written from a personal point of view, revealing both facts (though these may not be very objectively presented) and a person's feelings about them. In reading dance history, I've found biographies to be among the most enjoyable means of gaining knowledge. They tell an involving story and enable you to put yourself in someone else's shoes and judge how you would act and feel toward the events and situations described.

You can develop a feeling for dance's past as well as its present by reading historical material, and many books take you right up to the very near present. But bear in mind that concepts and theories about dance techniques and dance aesthetics change over time and vary from person to person. Be careful not to accept unquestioningly any one writer's point of view. Instead, compare and contrast it with other points of view and make your own judgment.

Below are listed some historical works to get you started:

HISTORY

Anderson, Jack. *Dance.* New York: Newsweek Books, 1974.

Clarke, Mary, and Clement Crisp. *Ballet: An Illustrated History.* New York: Universe Books, Inc., 1973.

Cohen, Selma Jeanne. *Dance as a Theatre Art.* New York: Dodd, Mead & Co., 1975.

———, editor. *Modern Dance: Seven Statements of Belief.* Middletown, Conn.: Wesleyan University Press, 1966.

DeMille, Agnes. *The Book of the Dance.* New York: Golden Press, 1963.

Duncan, Isadora. *The Art of the Dance.* New York: Theatre Arts Books, reprint of 1928 edition.

Guest, Ivor. *The Dancer's Heritage.* London: The Dancing Times, 1973.

Kirstein, Lincoln. *Dance: A Short History of Classical Theatrical Dancing.* New York: Dance Horizons, reprint of 1935 edition.

Martin, John. *Introduction to the Dance.* New York: Dance Horizons, reprint of 1939 edition.

Mazo, Joseph. *Prime Movers: The Makers of Modern Dance in America.* New York: William Morrow and Co., Inc., 1977.

McDonagh, Don. *The Rise and Fall and Rise of Modern Dance.* New York: New American Library, 1971.

BIOGRAPHY

Buckle, Richard. *Nijinsky.* New York: Simon and Schuster, 1971.

Cohen, Selma Jeanne. *Doris Humphrey: An Artist First.* Middletown, Conn.: Wesleyan University Press, 1972.

DeMille, Agnes. *Dance to the Piper.* New York: Grosset & Dunlap, 1951.

Guest, Ivor. *Fanny Elssler.* Middletown, Conn.: Wesleyan University Press, 1970.

McDonagh, Don. *Martha Graham.* New York: Praeger Publishers, Inc., 1973.

Terry, Walter. *Ted Shawn: Father of American Modern Dance.* New York: The Dial Press, 1976.

Reference Works

Just starting ballet? Or have you been in class for some time and now wonder about that word that sounds like "peekay"? A ballet dictionary will help. Various dance encyclopedias also are good for filling in definitions and details, not only about ballet but about other dance forms as well—even when they're entitled *An Encyclopedia* [or *Dictionary*] *of Ballet.* You can snatch a quick bit of information from them when you don't have time to plow through a book. You'll notice, though, that definitions in reference works may be different from each other and from your own teacher's, depending on stylistic interpretation and, in some cases, someone's just being plain wrong. Don't be surprised to find contrary ideas among writers, and between writers and dancers and teachers and choreographers.

Chujoy, Anatole, and P. W. Manchester. *The Dance Encyclopedia.* New York: Simon and Schuster, 1967.

Clarke, Mary, and David Vaughan. *The Encyclopedia of Dance and Ballet.* New York: G. P. Putnam's Sons, 1977.

Grant, Gail. *Technical Manual and Dictionary of Classical Ballet.* 2nd edition. New York: Dover Publications, 1967.

Koegler, Horst. *The Concise Oxford Dictionary of Ballet.* London, New York, and Toronto: Oxford University Press, 1977.

Mara, Thalia. *The Language of Ballet.* Cleveland and New York: The World Publishing Company, 1966.

Wilson, G. B. L. *Dictionary of Ballet.* New York: Theatre Arts Books, 1974.

Books about Dance Technique

There are quite a few instructional books about dance with information and ideas about the right way to do it. Many, unfortunately, are simply not good. I've tried to pinpoint the useful among them. There may be more that you can uncover for yourself by exploring libraries and bookstores and watching for newly published books. Be careful about using them, though. There's an enormous amount of misinformation published on the topic of dance.

Also remember that you can't learn to dance from a book. Although you can supplement your learning by reading, you must attend class.

BALLET

Hammond, Sandra Noll. *Ballet Basics.* Palo Alto, Calif.: National Press Books, 1974.

Vaganova, Agrippina. *Basic Principles of Classic Ballet: Russian Ballet Technique.* Tr. by Anatole Chujoy. New York: Dover Publications, 1969.

MODERN

Penrod, James, and Janice Gudde Plastino. *The Dancer Prepares*. Palo Alto, Calif.: Mayfield Publishing Co., 1970 (reprinted in 1977).

Sherbon, Elizabeth. *On the Count of One: Modern Dance Methods*. 2nd edition. Palo Alto, Calif.: Mayfield Publishing Co., 1975.

JAZZ

Cayou, Dolores Kirton. *Modern Jazz Dance*. Palo Alto, Calif.: Mayfield Publishing Co., 1971.

Sabatine, Jean. *Techniques and Styles of Jazz Dancing*. Waldwick, N.J.: Hoctor, 1969.

TAP

Ames, Jerry, and Jim Siegelman. *The Book of Tap*. New York: David McKay Co., 1977.

Audy, Robert. *Tap Dancing*. New York: Vintage Books, 1976.

Photographic Dance Books

Looking at photographs of dance can be more than just an enjoyable pastime—more than just relishing the beauty of line or the muscular definition of the subjects. A picture *is* worth a thousand words, and the meaning of all those corrections you've been hearing in class can come crashing through one day as you look at that one powerful dance photograph.

Photographs are two-dimensional, of course, and different from live dancing for that reason. But by the same token, and because they're presented as seen by the photographer's eye, they can give you new insight into technique, style, placement, and other such dance elements. Because a photograph catches and holds a shape, it allows you to linger over and examine it as you never could while watching a performance. Such an opportunity can at times be extremely useful to your own development as a dancer.

New dance photo books seem to be appearing in droves these

days, so you won't have any trouble finding them. Some that I particularly like are:

France, Charles Engell, editor. *Baryshnikov at Work*. New York: Alfred A. Knopf, 1976.

Kahn, Albert E. *Days with Ulanova*. New York: Simon and Schuster, 1962.

Leatherman, Le Roy. *Martha Graham*. Photographs by Martha Swope. New York: Alfred A. Knopf, 1966.

Mitchell, Jack. *Dance Scene: U.S.A.* Cleveland and New York: World Publishing Co., 1967.

Waldman, Max. *Waldman on Dance*. New York: William Morrow and Co., 1977.

Other Dance Books

There are, of course, many other books on dance than those mentioned here, and not all of them fall neatly into the categories I've set up. To attempt to list them would be like publishing a telephone directory. You can locate them through libraries and bookstores and will undoubtedly be able to recognize those that have particular meaning for you.

Anatomy and Physiology Books

Three special books on anatomy for dancers have been published within the past few years (they're listed below). As interest in dance grows, more are likely to appear. A knowledge of how the body is put together and how it works are important topics for dancers. This makes sense because we spend so much time attending to our bodies—exercising them, coaxing them to heal when injured, and demanding that they perform strenuous feats.

As you learned in Chapter 11, there's a school of thought that says you can have better control of your body if you have in mind an accurate picture of the body's composition—that is, where the bones and muscles are located and their relationship to each other. With such a picture, you can encourage your body to work more efficiently. To try out this theory, you may want to consider looking at some anatomy books to develop images of the body's muscles, bones, and joints.

Beyond its usefulness in building an accurate mental image of the body's components, a knowledge of anatomy may help you prevent injuries. If you understand how a joint is put together or how muscles in various parts of the body are placed, you're less likely to force them so far beyond their natural limits that they'll be injured. A knowledge of anatomy builds a kind of healthy respect for the body as a truly amazing feat of engineering. The more you learn about it, the more your admiration for it will grow and the better you'll know how to treat it.

You may at first be stunned by the technical terms in an anatomy book. They are in that less-than-popular language known as Latin, and even those for dancers and not medical students contain many of them. Don't let that deter you from your studies. Concentrate on the illustrations and on the text that you can understand, and don't worry about the Latin names. You can call your muscles by any names, so long as you know where they are and what they look like.

There aren't any physiology texts written especially for dancers, but a basic high-school or college text will give you information about body processes. Nutrition should be of primary concern to all dancers, and you'll usually find a chapter or two devoted to it in any basic physiology text.

ANATOMY

Gelabert, Raoul, and William Como. *Raoul Gelabert's Anatomy for the Dancer.* Vols. I & II. New York: Danad Publishing Co., Inc., 1964 and 1966.

Gray, Henry. *Anatomy of the Human Body.* Philadelphia: Lea and Febiger. Any edition.

Sparger, Celia. *Anatomy and Ballet.* 5th edition. London: Adam and Charles Black, 1970.

Sweigard, Lulu. *Human Movement Potential.* New York: Dodd, Mead & Co., 1974.

Todd, Mabel Elsworth. *The Thinking Body.* New York: Dance Horizons, reprint of 1937 edition.

PHYSIOLOGY

Sharkey, Brian J. *Physiology and Physical Activity.* New York: Harper & Row, 1975.

Dance Reviews

Louis Horst, the musician and composer who worked so closely with Martha Graham and who was also a critic, once published a review of a dance concert that was simply a blank column. While this was a novel way of reviewing a performance, it wasn't very considerate of the readers and dance enthusiasts who wanted to know something about the event. (Not to mention its lack of fairness to the choreographer and performers.) This type of reviewing is not common. Most critics make an honest attempt to inform their readers about what they see at a performance, what they think about it, and often how they place it in the development of dance as an art form. Of course, this is all presented from the critic's point of view, but if he or she has taken the time to become educated about dance, a review can be an excellent source of information as well as opinion.

Many major newspapers publish dance reviews on a regular basis or whenever there's a concert they think worthy of review. In New York, for instance, the *Times* publishes reviews almost daily and on Sundays, with more than one review following an evening in which more than one review-worthy concert occurred. For newspaper coverage of dance events in your city, see the *Dance Magazine Annual*, which lists local newspapers that regularly report on dance.

As dance gains in popularity, more local newspapers will hire reviewers to write about dance and will run general articles on dance. If your favorite newspaper hasn't yet reached that point, you might write a letter to the editor to prod him or her into action.

Magazines publish dance reviews from time to time, as well as special articles on dance. National magazines such as *Vogue*, *Harper's*, *Time*, and *Newsweek* have published reviews and articles (for example, features on dance personalities and dancing for fitness and health), and local magazines such as *New York* and *New West* make a practice of reviewing dance or featuring dance articles from time to time. Of course, *Dance Magazine* also publishes reviews.

Many reviews are collected and published in book form. These can be fine sources of background on dance and dance personalities. Some good collections are:

Croce, Arlene. *Afterimages*. New York: Alfred A. Knopf, 1977.
Denby, Edwin. *Looking at the Dance*. New York: Horizon Press, 1968.
Jowitt, Deborah. *Dance Beat*. New York: Marcel Dekker, Inc., 1977.
Reynolds, Nancy. *Repertory in Review*. New York: The Dial Press, 1977.
Siegel, Marcia. *At the Vanishing Point*. New York: Saturday Review Press, 1968–72.
———. *Watching the Dance Go By*. Boston: Houghton Mifflin, 1977.

Magazines Devoted to Dance

The best-known magazine in America devoted to dance is *Dance Magazine*. It's distributed nationally and available at newsstands and in libraries in most major cities. In it you'll find reviews, articles, and news about dance and dancers, a calendar of events covering major dance performances nationally, a school directory, and advertisements from dance schools and dance-supply stores throughout the country. The *Dance Magazine Annual* is a special issue that organizes information about dance and dance resources and can be extraordinarily useful to students and others interested in dance.

Other magazines devoted to dance, although less ambitious in their coverage, offer excellent articles.

Ballet Review, Box 639, Brooklyn, N.Y. 11202.
Dance Magazine, 10 Columbus Circle, New York, N.Y. 10019.
Dance News, 119 West 57th Street, New York, N.Y. 10019.
Dance Perspectives, 29 East 9th Street, New York, N.Y. 10003.
Dance Scope, American Dance Guild, Suite 603, 1619 Broadway, New York, N.Y. 10019.
Eddy, 124 Chambers Street, New York, N.Y. 10007.

Libraries

Most dancers don't have unlimited income with which to go out and buy all the books and magazines mentioned thus far. And that is where public and school libraries can come in very handy. Since New York is the dance capital of the world, it follows that the best library facility devoted to dance in the Unites States is located there: the Lincoln Center Library for the Performing Arts Dance Collection. Headed by Genevieve Oswald, the collection houses books, periodicals, photographs, taped interviews, films, and other material. It also maintains files of clippings on dancers, dance companies, choreographers, composers, and dance-related topics and personalities. A ten-volume catalogue of the collection tells you everything that's in it and is regularly updated with additions on microfiche.

The librarians who staff the Dance Collection are an exceptional breed who take pride in their work and seem to relish the opportunity to help you. If you go there, you may also be lucky enough to see one of your dance idols sitting quietly at one of the small movie screens in the room, viewing the filmed version of a role he or she is learning. Dance writers are also familiar faces at the Dance Collection. There have been few visits during which I haven't seen a dance personality or two or at least one dancer friend.

The Dance Collection is purely for reference purposes, so you can't take out any books. Just downstairs in the Lincoln Center Library building, though, is the circulating dance collection, from which you can borrow books if you have a New York Public Library card.

Branches in many public library systems usually have some books on dance, either in the reference section or in the circulating collection. If a circulating book you want isn't on the shelf, remember that you can ask that it be reserved for you when it's returned. In many libraries this means a nominal investment in a reply post card at the main desk.

The quality of dance-book collections of libraries in smaller cities and in high schools, colleges, and universities will vary. Some will be totally barren, owning not a single book or magazine dealing with dance. Others will present a feast filling several shelves. The librarian often has a lot to say about what books and magazines are ordered for the library and, if you request one or two, may actually purchase them with the next available budget money. (Although you may be far off and well on your way toward stardom by that time, at least you'll have made your contribution to the development of the collection for future dancers.)

Bookstores

In New York City a few stores specialize in dance books and usually welcome browsers. Other cities may not be lucky enough to have specialized sales outlets, but you can usually look around freely in any bookstore. Besides, you may want to do some buying as well as browsing. Even if you're on a tight budget, some books are really worth the splurge. They can be a lifelong source of pleasure and inspiration that you can always turn to in solitary moments and that you can share with friends and fellow dancers in sociable times.

For places that specialize in dance books, look in the *Dance Magazine Annual* under "Sources of Dance Books," or in other issues of the magazine where these stores may advertise. You may also ask at any ordinary bookstore if they know of a place that stocks books on dance, or ask your teacher to recommend one. Keep in mind that dance books can often be found in the art, theater, or music section of a general bookstore.

Dance Performances

You'll never have a problem finding a place to see dance if you live in New York City. Your only problem will be choosing which places to go. There are so many New York-based companies and so many others that come to New York to perform that there's almost no evening in which a concert isn't scheduled.

Cities outside of New York can't yet support as great a number or as wide a variety of dance performances as New York. But each year interest in dance grows, causing more local companies to spring up and companies that tour to be asked to perform in more locales. Such performances and special dance events are usually heralded well enough in advance so that you may plan to attend.

You can keep up with dance events in a number of ways. Newspapers run ads about upcoming performances, and many also publish an "arts calendar" that lists music, theater, and dance. You can also check the calendar in each issue of *Dance Magazine*, which covers dance performances across the country. Radio and television advertising is becoming more widely used for dance, and you'll also see announcements and ads in fliers you'll receive in the mail once your name gets on a dance mailing list or two.

The more concerts you attend and performances you subscribe to, the better are your chances of becoming firmly entrenched in the dance world's mailing lists. If you can afford them, most major professional companies offer subscriptions for their seasons or their series of performances when they're on tour. If there are companies you'd particularly like to see, you may be able to place your name on their mailing lists by letting them know of your interest when you attend one of their performances (ask at the box office) or by contacting their administrative office directly by mail or phone (look in the program for information on their management and where they're located).

For dance or arts organizations that sponsor dance events in your city, check the *Dance Magazine Annual* under the headings "Community Arts Councils" and "State, Regional and Local Organizations Sponsoring Dance." These groups support dance in various ways. For instance, in New York City the Theatre Development Fund (TDF)[27] allows you to see some performances for $1 if you buy a set of TDF "Dance Vouchers" ($5 for a set of five). Once you buy these, your name goes on a mailing list and you also receive a calendar that keeps you posted on New York's dance happenings.

The experience of seeing dance is so obviously important to any dance student that I haven't yet bothered to toot any horns about it. Once you've seen live dance, no one has to tell you about its value. It provides dynamic lessons in technique and expressiveness. It inspires you in your own studies. It can plant ideals in your heart that you never imagined in your wildest dreams and turn the lights onto what all those exercises you do in class are about. In a recent interview Louis Falco (formerly of the Jose Limon company and now with a group of his own) reflected on his in-class experience:

> I hadn't even seen Martha Graham at that time, although we were taught Graham technique. We sat on the floor and did contractions hour after hour. Only when I saw the Graham company . . . did I realize, "Oh, this is what you end up doing."[28]

Films and Television

Films and television tapes of dance have different dynamic effects than live dance performances. They're often separated into art forms in themselves, being two- rather than three-dimensional and presenting views that are selected by director, cameraperson, and editor rather than by audience. That issue aside, they are valuable resources for the dance student. A recent series called *Dance in America*, produced by the educational station in New York City, WNET–Channel 13, had the added attraction of comments by the company directors and other well-known personalities which enhanced the viewer's understanding of the choreographers' goals and intents. In another program WNET presented live the ballet *Giselle*, starring Mikhail Baryshnikov and Natalia Makarova; it also included an interview with Erik Bruhn at intermission. It was a history-making and thrilling event to watch.

Announcements of television shows are run in the newspapers and are often specially advertised by the stations. When dance films are shown at movie houses, they will usually be advertised in the newspapers. Some public libraries show dance films as part of their community activities program. And you can see the Lincoln Center Dance Collection's films by making a reservation with the librarian (telephone 799-2200).

Bulletin Boards

Almost every dance studio you take classes in will have a bulletin board or a wall on which notices will be posted. Usually you'll find announcements about auditions, performances, classes, and special courses. You're also likely to see messages from masseurs, choreographers who want some dancers to work with, people who knit warm-up tights, and students who want to sell new pointe shoes that don't quite fit (at a reduced price).

Dancers who need roommates and people who rent studio space will use the board as an information center, too.

Make it a habit to look over any bulletin boards you see in dance studios. You never know when you'll catch sight of an audition for a company you'd like to join or some other tidbit that will be important or at least interesting to you.

Talking to Dancers, Dance Teachers, and Other People

Depending on how outgoing a person you are, approaching strangers may be a breeze or a gargantuan effort. If you're somewhat shy, you'll find it's well worth steeling yourself to overcome your natural reticence, for talking to dancers, teachers, and other people can open a treasury of dance information.

Where you are in your development as a dancer will often determine the types of information you'll be seeking in your conversations. As a beginner you may have very basic questions (for example, should you study ballet, modern, jazz, or tap?), and you may not even be sure what questions to start with. Chapter 1 in this book should help you, and remember that once you've thrown out the first question, you've invited a conversation that could sprout some productive answers and possible new friendships.

Of course you should give thought to the likeliness of the candidates you elect to address your questions to. Certainly other dance students are good sources. But if you haven't yet begun classes, you can try asking among your friends to see if they know any dance students or teachers. With the growing population of dancers, it's highly likely they'll deliver someone. Ask in the building where you live, or where you work, or when you are at a party. (I haven't been to any parties lately where at least one other dancer hasn't made an appearance.)

Studio dressing rooms are excellent places to ask questions and also to eavesdrop. (I've found several good teachers by noting casual remarks made by other dancers who were donning leotards and tights along with me.) You can learn about classes, teachers, auditions, performances, where to buy dance clothes cheaply, and many other useful topics in the dressing room. You'll also hear theories about injuries and nutrition, some of which may be accurate and others which you'll want to blot out of your mind immediately. As with any information that is important to you—that may seriously affect your career, your health, or your general well-being—you should be careful to evaluate it before putting it to use.

Timid about approaching the teacher with a question? Don't be. Most dance teachers are on the job to impart skill and information. A question from you, especially after class or at a time when it won't disrupt the flow of class events, gives your teacher the chance to fulfill a natural function. Most will respond warmly and as fully as they can. You should ask your teacher questions about class, a particular step or combination, technique in general, your progress, your career goals, or any other dance-related topic that's of concern or interest to you.

Keep a sharp eye out in class for students whose dancing you especially like. You may want to ask where else they study or what types of dance have contributed to their present dance ability. Natural talent is always a factor, of course, but you still need to acquire your basic technique somewhere.

Talking to other students may also open some doors for you. One of my first chances to perform occurred when I became friendly with a tall, quiet, dark-haired woman in class who turned out to be the choreographer Toby Armour. I performed with her and then later, after she'd introduced me to him, with James Waring. A well-placed, well-timed question to the right person just might lead you down a path to some golden dance opportunities.

14

A Spark That Shines:
Individuality in Dancing

His is not the kind of body that will twist into a pretzel or bend double and inside out. It is a typically masculine body—solid and a bit tight in the hips. There is no use trying to make him into a twisting mosquito. Who wants to see one, anyway? Solidity can be a limitation that works as an asset.

—Paul Taylor [29]

This book has been about individuality. It has been about taking the specific action that will lead you to find yourself as a dancer.

No two dancers, like no two people, are ever totally alike; to understand this concept, respect it, and learn how to maximize it is at the core of becoming a complete and expressive dancer.

In our present mass-produced world, it's often difficult to keep sight of the value of uniqueness and even harder to find space where it may grow. Dancing can provide an excellent environment for it, perhaps one of the few remaining universal contexts for it, if you will allow yourself the luxury and encourage the development of the dancer who is you and you alone.

When we look at some of the traditional ballets in the classical repertory, it's easy to see how we can be led astray from the ideal of individual expressiveness in dance. We watch a dozen swans in *Swan Lake*, for example, and we think to ourselves, Isn't it wonderful! They're all the same size, their arms are all rounded in the same pretty circles, and their hair is all neatly tucked into their identical headpieces. Or we go to see the Rockettes, and all the dancers look like sisters. How can we ever forget that line of legs, all the same length, kicking at exactly the same precise moment, to the same exact height? We say to ourselves, Aha! So this is what dancing must be about.

Of course, we're also aware of the ballerinas and the soloists, as in the outside world we're aware of millionaires and movie stars. But we think of them as the exceptions; and while in our imagination we may dream of ourselves in such a unique place, most of us in our more practical moments think of the exception as someone else.

Training in dance also may appear to emphasize conformity and sameness. There are standards of technique and aesthetics that unquestionably affect the conduct of dance classes. As students, we strive to meet the standards set forth by our teachers, and are reinforced with praise when we do.

Many of the jobs dancers have open to them these days require more sameness than individuality. After all, how many stars can there be in one show? Choreographers, particularly in profit-oriented Broadway shows, prefer dancers who will "fit."

There's something called a "type" audition, in which you don't have to dance at all. You just put your body up for inspection, and if it's the right size and has the right look to blend with the other bodies that have already been selected, you're automatically in the running for the job.

It's easier for some people than it is for others to fall into line, to consistently fill the role and fit the bill. They're just born with more standard equipment or have learned better how to make themselves appear that way. Nevertheless, each of us has a spark of uniqueness that wants to shine. And by denying it we can wind up in Pete Seeger's "Little Boxes," looking out through the same windows at the same dismal view as everyone else. We can drain our creative energies and sap our natural strength for life by putting all our efforts into shaping up to what we're supposed to be.

It shouldn't have to take courage to acknowledge and cultivate the qualities that are special in each of us. All around us, though, are recognition and rewards for conforming, and it takes stamina to fly in their face. I firmly believe, however, that your dance training, like your life, can be more productive and happier if you admit to your own uncommonness. Even if you happen to fit in size-wise, color-wise, age-wise, and otherwise with the chorus, and you're ecstatically happy to be making money in the line, I think that you'll still benefit from and be better off recognizing yourself as an individual—that you can get the most from your dance training and your existence by using that recognition in constructive ways.

Taking class with an eye turned toward your individuality and your special needs is a delicate matter, but one that's possible to handle. Essentially, when you go to class you are agreeing to occupy the same space, spend the same block of time, follow the instructions of the same teacher, and go through the same series of exercises as all the other students in the class. The trick is to coordinate the particular needs of your own body and personality with what is offered in the general class environment.

It's amazing to think that such an event can actually come to pass for all the different people in class. It is possible, though, to participate harmoniously in the general activities of the class and at the same time keep track of your personal needs and objectives.

Beyond the minimum definition of the technical level of a class—beginner, intermediate, and so on—finding what you need in the situation depends on recognizing your objectives and being alert to conditions under which they're not being met. Your objectives may range from improving a particular dance step to strengthening a weak part of your body. Or you may be concerned first and foremost with working on good alignment. Or you may find it imperative to increase your sense of movement. If you're a beginner, you may want to focus on getting in touch with sensations in your body.

Of course, your teacher will set objectives that he or she considers important for you and the rest of the class. Ideally, these should come close to your own. But it's inevitable that they won't in all cases. You must somehow stay aware of objectives that are different from those stressed in class, and not get caught up in activities that don't lead toward your goals.

Suppose, for instance, that one of your aims is to learn how to breathe well while you're moving. The class is in the midst of an exercise designed to build strength and stamina and requiring much effort. As you perform the exercise you notice that you're straining like crazy and taking in barely any oxygen. Is it a sin to stop doing the exercise or cut out one or two repetitions of it? If it's not disruptive to the class and you feel that building strength and stamina are secondary to learning how to breathe, then you have a legitimate reason not to do for a moment or two what everybody else is doing.

Of course, if you find that this happens quite often in a class, then you'll have to examine whether the general objectives of the class coincide closely enough with your own for you to continue. Perhaps a slower class or different environment will be better for you. Within reasonable limits, however, and provided it doesn't interfere with the conduct and flow of class, you can work on the goals you have set for yourself.

Sometimes a type of dance and a class may match your objectives almost precisely, but there'll be an emphasis every now and again that simply shouldn't have very much importance for you. For example, suppose you're taking tap class just for the fun of it. You've been at it about eight or nine months and are having a ball. In class tonight you've just learned a dizzying, flashy step and are delighted with your accomplishment. Before you can do it a second time, the teacher has put another frill on it, and when you try it you find your feet smashing into each other and your tongue shooting spastically out of your mouth. You repeat it several times with the same results. Remember, you're in this to have fun! You can do the step perfectly fine without the extra frill. Why should you forget your original intent and change it from enjoying yourself to killing yourself?

To be true to yourself as a dancer, you must keep perspective on the situations you're in and on your own needs, not sacrificing the latter for the former. It's up to you to pick and choose among the commitments you'll make; you really do have the power to decide for yourself.

If you've concentrated on all the individual factors I've talked about in this book, you're well on your way to letting your body express itself in its own unique way—whether it's a prima ballerina assoluta, a musical-comedy dancer, or an accountant who loves to go to jazz class for relaxation after a long, hard day of looking at numbers. If you experiment thoughtfully with techniques, teachers, classes, and schools and keep open the channels of communication between your head and your body, you're likely to arrive at a place where your dancing is very specially your own. You will be an active participant in the choices that determine how successfully and expressively you'll live with your dancing.

It's the differences among all of us that make the dancing we do so exciting and full of discoveries. The ways we look, our tastes, our movement preferences—all of the elements that make up our individual physiques and personalities—add up to the variety that is truly the spice of our dancing. Don't deny yourself and those who may watch you the pleasure of the unique physical and spiritual being that you are—of your individuality and your completeness as a dancer.

1. Joyce Wadler, "Tap Your Troubles Away." *New York Post*, February 5, 1977, magazine section, p. 21.
2. Barry Tarshis, *The Creative New Yorker*. New York: Simon and Schuster, 1972.
3. Evelyn de La Tour, "Education Comes Dancing," in *Dance—An Art in Academe*, edited by Martin Haberman and Tobie Meisel. New York: Teachers' College Press, 1970.
4. Tobi Tobias, "It's Becoming Okay in America for Boys to Dance." *New York Times*, Arts and Leisure section, January 9, 1977, p. 6.
5. Ernestine Stodelle, "Reflections on the 1959 Conference of Creative Teaching of Dance to Children." *Dance Observer*, Vol. 27, No. 5, May 1960, p. 71.
6. See the excellent article by Nancy Goldner, "The School of American Ballet," in Nancy Reynolds's *Repertory in Review*. New York: The Dial Press, 1977.

   Agnes de Mille's *To a Young Dancer* (Boston: Little, Brown, 1962) and Regina Woody's *Young Dancer's Career Book* (New York: E. P. Dutton, 1958) contain some dated information, but much of it still applies.

   And see Chapter 13 of this book for other suggestions.
7. In New York City, look for listings in the *Poor Dancer's Almanac, A Guide to Living and Dancing in New York*. New York: Association of

American Dance Companies, 162 West 56th Street, New York, N.Y. 10019.

8. You might try a book entitled *Nutriscore* by Ruth Fremes and Dr. Zak Sabry (Toronto and New York: Methuen/Two Continents, 1976), which gives nutrition information and provides a "scorebook" in which you can keep track of your nutritional intake. Or look for *Nutrition Almanac* by Nutrition Search, Inc., John D. Kirschmann, Director (New York: McGraw-Hill, 1973 and 1975), which also enables you to compute your nutritional intake and needs.

9. Brian Sharkey, *Physiology and Physical Activity*. New York: Harper and Row, 1975.

10. Data for table from Barbara Kraus, *Calories and Carbohydrates*. New York: Signet Books, 1975.

11. See Lulu Sweigard, *Human Movement Potential*. New York: Dodd, Mead & Co., 1974.

12. See Mabel Elsworth Todd, *The Thinking Body*. New York: Dance Horizons, 1937 (reprinted in 1975).

13. Sweigard, op. cit.

14. Todd, op. cit.

15. Irene Dowd, "Finding Your Center." *Eddy*, Winter 1977, No. 9 p. 5.

16. See Daniel Arnheim, *Dance Injuries: Their Prevention and Care*. St. Louis: The C. V. Mosby Co., 1975.

17. Haynes Owens is the author of the metaphors and most of the images mentioned.

18. Mikhail Baryshnikov, "Working: A Preface," in *Baryshnikov at Work*, edited by Charles Engell France. New York: Alfred A. Knopf, 1976, 1976, p. 8.

19. Alan Richardson, "Mental Practice: A Review and Discussion." *Research Quarterly* 38, March and September 1967, pp. 95–107, 263–273.

20. Haynes Owens is the author of most of the images mentioned.

21. Sweigard, op. cit.

22. *Dance Magazine Directory of College and University Dance*. New York: Danad Publishing Co., 1976. (A revised edition is projected for 1978.)

23. *Dance Magazine* and *Dance Magazine Annual*, 10 Columbus Circle, New York, N.Y. 10019.

24. *Dance Magazine* and *Dance Magazine Annual*, 10 Columbus Circle, New York, N.Y. 10019.

25. See the *Dance Magazine Annual* or ask for information from the Association of American Dance Companies, 162 West 56th Street, New York, N.Y. 10019. If you decide to live in New York City, life can be easier if you buy a copy of the *Poor Dancer's Almanac* (see note 7 above).

26. The American Dance Guild *Newsletter* is sent to members. Someone in almost every dance department belongs. American Dance Guild, 1619 Broadway, New York, N.Y. 10019. For other career possibilities, you may also want to consult Walter Terry's *Careers for the Seventies: Dance*. New York: Crowell-Collier Press, 1971.

27. Theatre Development Fund, Room 2110, 1501 Broadway, New York, N.Y. 10036.

28. Anna Kisselgoff, "I Would Love to Create Earthquakes Onstage." *New York Times*, Arts and Leisure section, April 10, 1977, p. 8.

29. Paul Taylor describing Dan Wagoner in "Down with Choreography" in *Modern Dance: Seven Statements of Belief*, edited by Selma Jeanne Cohen. Middletown, Conn.: Wesleyan University Press, 1966.